I0366846

FREDDY SNAKES
MĀRATOPIA

Freddy Snakes
- Māratopia -

First Edition published in Māratopia County by Fatback Books, 2022
Copyright © Freddy Snakes, 2022
ISBN 978-1-5272-8332-9

All rights reserved.
No part of this book may be reproduced in any form without permission in writing from the publisher, except by a reviewer who may quote brief passages in a review to be printed in a magazine or newspaper.

visit:
freddysnakes.com

Front Cover Artwork: Ink Bad Company

LA CRESTA VILLAGE
MĀRATOPIA

CONTENTS

1. SELVIN — 1
2. MY HEART SKIPPED... — 3
3. SASKIA AMOS — 5
4. SAN COTTON — 13
5. BERTHA TEXIROSA — 17
6. LÉGUVAN TIGGS — 37
7. SEVENTH SEAL SOCIETY CHURCH — 43
8. SARATOKA PLAINS — 57
9. ZEKE MORAY — 81
10. JOHNNY SNAKES — 97
11. JESSE RAPIER — 105
12. REBELLION, DEATH, AND BLACK MAGIC — 113
13. MASHED INTO THE SUN-BEATEN GROUND — 119
14. DAISY LITTLELEAF — 121
15. HIGH AS A SCREAMING DIAMOND — 129
16. RICKY SNAKES — 133
17. TOMBSTONE SKULL — 141
18. SCARECHILD — 145
19. ROCCA DEL CULTO — 149
20. REST IN PEACE OLD FRIEND — 151
21. MORE MADDER AND MAGICAL THAN EVER — 153
22. THE PLAYGROUND — 159
23. MAD MICKY NOLAN — 165

Introduction

With the aim of tracing my path through the fire, like silver tried seven times, allow this novel/memoir to standout as a snapshot of my life and its fiery trials. I came into this realm *from the bosom of the perfect thought,* to manifest in flesh for the explicit purpose of learning how to overcome, detach, and most importantly, to learn how to love.

My story is for the warrior soul; the one moving from disorder to order (from one life-changing incident to another)—passing into higher states of consciousness and wisdom and freedom. My story is a hallucinatory, raw, beautiful, real, truthful, surreal sacrifice: all the parts of my soul I am willing to bear, like a gaping wound of mighty silence.

*It is to be noted, when consciousness occupies an avatar (in this training simulator called Earth), an opportunity to learn and to grow wise, is, the chance to *find a way outta here*. And while some warriors have been cut down too soon, others, losing their path, have fallen for the trick, that all of this is real. But the wide awake ones, they know that all of this is only a game, as they continue to get stronger, never ceasing to learn, always seeking peace in their current life—*in order to* attract peace in the next life.

And so as one ascends (in their current life and onto the next one) one is forever learning who they truly are, being as it is, a requirement of the soul (minus the attachment to desire) to release more and more the things that once weighed it down. Hence, why forgiveness of self and others, i.e. love of self and others, is the highest form of detachment, and the key to ascension.

My story you could say, is a headstone to my old life. A life that peacefully I have laid to rest. A life that was a stepping stone to more fulfilled, abundant, richer experiences.

Therefore; I am grateful to all the legends and influencers—including the mad, crazy missions that made me back then, who I needed to be now: just another vessel, responsible for carrying a message to whoever may find it useful, at some far-off point down the line.

Freddy Snakes

Welcome to Māratopia County,
home of the wild spirit,
a place you enter at your own peril,
cos once you decide to cross that line and step
into Māratopia,
it can mean only one thing -
no more compromise,
as now true to yourself,
you are found standing your ground in a fight
for what is pure and good.

In Māratopia County
you can be whatever you want -
so step-up and be one of the courageous,
a pioneer, a visionary, a healer,
one of the chosen -
born 'n' raised ready to burn;
free and fierce,
brave enough to run with it
and go out brightly lit.

This is the genuine heart of Māratopia County,
a place where its people are its treasure.

Māratopia, a world where legends roam.

Māratopìa

HOME OF THE WILD SPIRIT

A WORLD WHERE LEGENDS ROAM

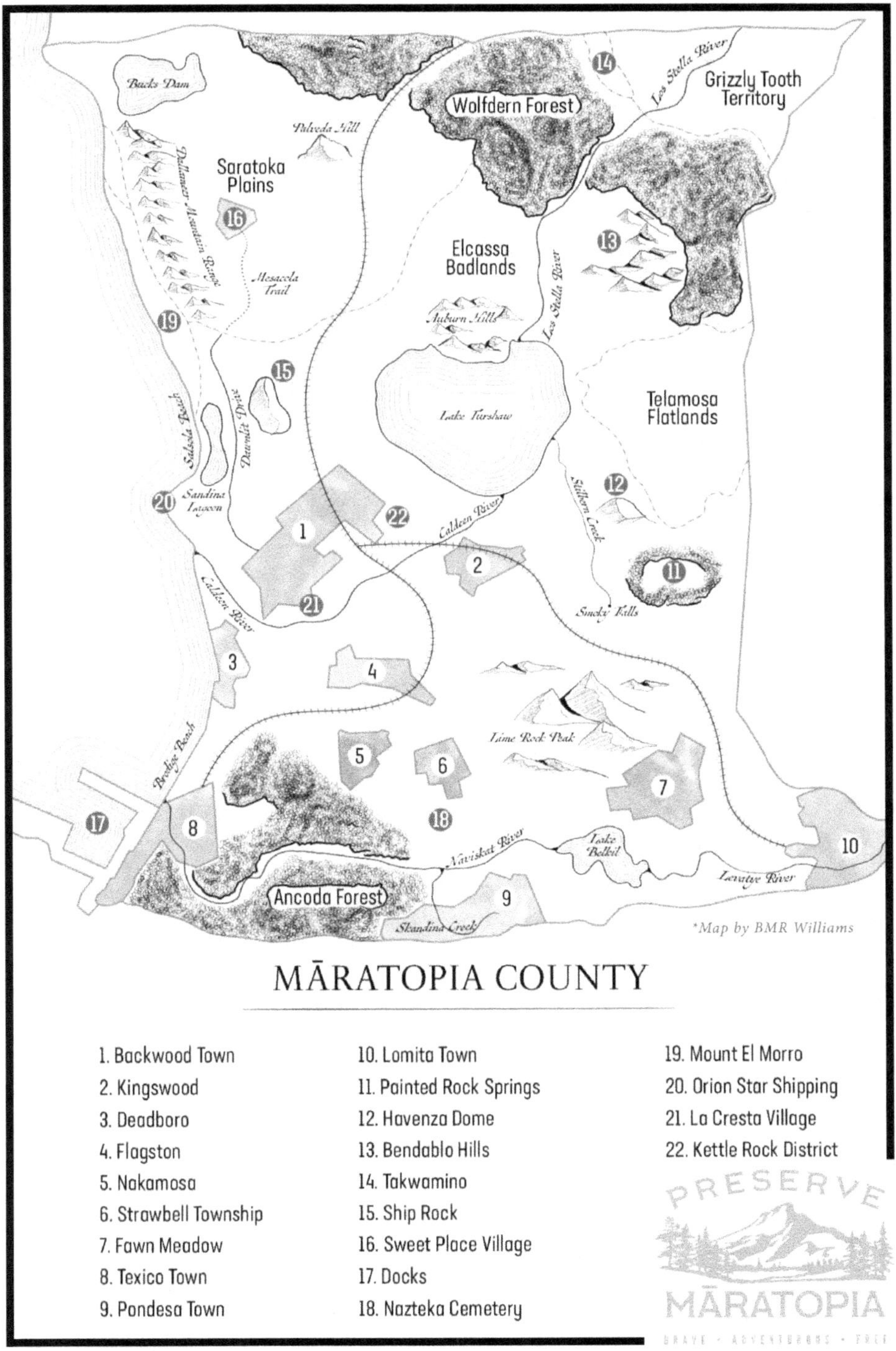

MĀRATOPIA COUNTY

1. Backwood Town
2. Kingswood
3. Deadboro
4. Flagston
5. Nakamosa
6. Strawbell Township
7. Fawn Meadow
8. Texico Town
9. Pondesa Town
10. Lomita Town
11. Painted Rock Springs
12. Havenza Dome
13. Bendablo Hills
14. Takwamino
15. Ship Rock
16. Sweet Place Village
17. Docks
18. Nazteka Cemetery
19. Mount El Morro
20. Orion Star Shipping
21. La Cresta Village
22. Kettle Rock District

PRESERVE MĀRATOPIA
BRAVE · ADVENTUROUS · FREE

THIS IS A TRUE STORY

" A LIFE OF REBIRTH
ON THE OPEN ROAD,
IS TRUE MEDICINE
TO A WISE MAN. "
- FREDDY SNAKES -

1.

SELVIN

I knew him from previous Amarantium Viotriptamine scores, as he stood *leaned up* in the doorway of the El Mosca—corner of 22nd and L'Shasta Street, Backwood, Māratopia.

The El Mosca: a corner shop-cum-takeaway—was thee focal hangout for the town's local dope merchants—majority of them all "Jawheads"—suitable slang; given the old school ghetto drug: "Nitrope"—they all smoked by means of the "purple pipe". 'Cos when you hit a pipe, brachie, you feel all horny and lush in a dreamy kinda way.'

And amongst "Nitrope" users, the common greeting is: "What's good y'all, make a pipe, why dontcha."—executed by taking an empty quart-bottle by the neck and smashing it on a brick. Then, taking a gerrick or diamond or rather a purple pipe filter made from cardboard or cigarette foil rolled into a coil, jam it into the bottle mouth, but not too tight as the pipe must pull smooth.

NEXT—load the neck up with *"Plug"*—the nastiest dead ass weed you can find. *Scrub or ragweed* they call it - low-grade back-alley weed—no sense torching your supergrade on a purple pipe; the ragweed is just a medium for burning and inhaling the Nitrope, or what rocket scientists in white overcoats call: cyclindicyde or Lindies: a pharmaceutical sleeping tab used in the early '60s but soon taken off the market due to its high addiction rate.

Now after you're done stuffing the pipe - take a tab of Nitrope—wrap it in a bank note—lay a flat blade over it and bash it with your fist so it's proper crushed. Then sprinkle the purple powder—coating the top of the pipe with "the cream".

Remember to keep a bucket handy, as you may feel the urge to bark up a lung or drool or vomit after you're done hitting that pipe.

Then once you're all SET—squat down near that bucket—get one of your *pals* to fire up three matches and bust that pipe *brachie*—sucking it in goood—filling your chest with that thick, acrid smoke—frying up lungs like burger meat on take-out night. But beware, for clenching onto that drug you're gonna to get a billion volt charge that's gonna blast your balls off and make you rush like a motherfucker. The sensation like a hit of Psychatrosis while peaking on three Xycamorphinol tabs—only though a lot meaner and more intense—recalling the first time I "pulled" on a "purple pipe": my skull blew its flap—steam whistle style, while in a hot and cold wince, my brains; cooked up, crooned like a pink-ass baboon frothin' at the gills—muscles cranking spasms as all I could do was spit, drool and die—hugging onto that blessed bucket for dear life.

AFTERWARDS—feeling woozy—melting into slippery sweats I collapsed zoned-out into a euphoric zombie-like state that wore off pretty quick. And to remain high I would've had to have hit that pipe again. But instead spent the whole windy day miserable, awake and used-up.

And so the addicts I hung out with did this "Ritual for the Lost" daily—selling scrap metal to keep their habit on the back boiler. But the dope merchants that operated in and around Backwood they were a completely different matter. They fuelled their addiction earning buckskins by selling bad drugs to naive casual users. Palming stuff off like stale Amarantium Viotriptamine (a powerful hallucinogen) and fake Xycamorphinol or "Ether" (a strong love drug). Even flea powder as Proloxytin or "Fizz" (a loud simulant - commonly snorted). But on that particular night, in the angelic doorway, stood the ever radiant Selvin.

2.

MY HEART SKIPPED ...

I bought "trips" off Selvin before—fresh, dazzling merchandise. He being thee most trusted mert in Backwood. Working directly for the cultists—who supplied the streets with real spine-chilling "trips". The kind of stuff the Los Rucās and Ravedas bugged-out on.

The year was 1995 and the dawning of a "Goodbye" for the once potent Los Rucā and Raveda scene. Star Culture having now bloomed into something marketable; after three years gathering disciples at a ritualistic level: first at illegal word-of-mouth forest venues, and then abandoned warehouses, to later—high street clubs, and onward to bigger sponsored weekends of losing oneself. The '90s turning out to be the last classic decade on earth.

And so now those that in the late eighties and early nineties who religiously dropped "Amarantium", and dressed in black, and dyed their hair black, and wore black eyeliner. By a single crack of midnight lightning, they morphed like hive-minded hornets into an alien tribe of gum-smacking, broke-jawed, asexual, peroxided creeps, all popping and chomping "Xycamorphinol's", like kiddies binging on Love Hearts candy. The lot of 'em GONE—grinding tense teeth—no longer coherent enough even to lineup a sentence; their brains like mashed testicles (quite fascinating to behold), as they crawled the so-called walls with eyes rolled back brilliantly into their sockets - their souls ruddy—melting within porcelain skin; cold as lizard gloves, being HIT to the stars on this popular drug. The lot of 'em, radiating like newborns with bright laughing smiles and eyes shining love.

A new generation this was, full of positive direction and drug-dipped dawn. Seen now in starry-eyed queues—hanging outside throbbing nightclubs. Girls with *bodies beautiful* radiating love, and sex-for-free. Faces sprayed in glitter. Eyes painted. Lashes beating hummingbird flirtation. Skins aflutter with candy perfume—as dressed in screaming tights, Lycra hot pants, micro mini's, and breathtaking cleavage tops... Keen 10/10 girls earned fast reputations and celeb-like status. And as for the guys? Those once serious, hard-edged, don't-fuck-with-me heavy metal blokes, they came like fresh lambs to a new slaughter; all with g-cuts and faces shaven, splashed to the gargle in cream soda cologne. All of 'em like lovers lit up with drug-doused grins; sniggering like first time lovers - dressed in tight neon tees, silver pants and booted in All-Stars and skate shoes. The lot of 'em CHILDREN of the X-generation now.

* * *

It was a Sunday night. Everything stood still. The clubs closed. The streets empty. 22nd and Lowland Street dead. Nothing except old news tumbled through town. Not a fortunate soul about, just drunk vagrants and bare-foot, snot-nosed orphans high on glue.

I approached the bristling figure in the doorway. It flickered like a familiar flame. Its posture reminding me of thunders framed in flashes. A vessel containing an authentically stained soul. A reposed figure torn and tarnished with a vibrant aura - holding a pocketful of keys to numerous portals—smiling a sexy passion gap while nodding and acknowledging my return to buy more blood, guts, and glory.

My heart skipped like a schoolgirl without a care in the world. The WORD being: "double-coated gold Starfalls": pellets of Amarantium the size-of-a plastic headed pin. It was enough. I would need only three. I paid the money and got handed three tiny pieces of foil paper. My outer-pilgrimage, en route!

3.

SASKIA AMOS

MISSION on track, I walked back to Dawnlit Drive (a 5.4 mile stretch from the outskirts of Saratoka Plains into the heart of Backwood) and stood there smoking my Joey Jim Blues; hitching a ride back home.

Now hitchhiking in Māratopia, for both driver and lone drifter poised along the dimly lit roadside is a two-sided affair, as one cannot be too sure of thoe who prowl this tormented landscape and its darkest hour. And life sure knows I've had my pure share of creeps. Dudes offering blowjobs. Predators looking to unleash a barrage of perversion on some poor unsuspecting ass. Sick vultures: old cruisers: rich pervos—cruising to pick a boy's bones clean. Recalling one old cruiser in a mustard yellow '83 Lotus Esprit, who tried to soften me, getting into my head with ideas of going into town to pick up girls at The Lounge Bar; down on L'Shasta Street. And with these girls back at his penthouse we'd party and snort lines, hit weed and get naked—sipping bubbly in his Jacuzzi *all* with the aim of screwing these imaginary nymphs, which piqued my interest, as he *all the while* milked the game—keeping his wheezing eye upon me—licking his lips—waiting to glimpse the moment I succumbed to his snare; carrying on as he did, gesturing about The Lounge Bar—emphasizing the elongated phallic-like symbols that were part of the décor—suggesting I'd feel right at home, being a sensitive poet-and-all, you know the type that's all hung-up on finding the core diamond of degrangment deep within the "epic mission", along with loss of self—my passion for writing and mind-expanding drugs a topic we touched on earlier, as we got pretty deep—my fault—slipping guard—being too polite and naive—allowing it to carry-on as far as it did, as he, all the while, spouting bad-steam like a doctor of carnal wisdoms, dealt cards like a diseased man to whom time meant nothing—playing me like a fucking game—all-in-all—the underlying gnashing-of-teeth truth BEING that he fancied boys and wanted to pop my ass cherry and ram his swollen knob so far up my colon I'd be biting the bullet, pleading: 'Sweet Jezem!' as he doused my fire in old boy's cream. And so as we sat there pulled-off in the dark, the subject of weed cropped up, his window of opportunity; I guess, as he asked: 'So handsome, where do you keep your weed, tucked under your balls?' a clear come on, shivering with disease as he said the word "balls".

Meanwhile, all that time in my coat pocket I had a firm grasp on my axe, just in case, ready for that dirty old fuck to make the wrong move, which lucky for his sake, he didn't.

On the other end of the hitchhiking spectrum, I recall the Devilish-duo... A couple of pure "hellers" on a death ride to meet-their-maker - fully prepared for their last take-off into the surging sun. And it was just a matter of wrong time, wrong place that saw me locked into that metal coffin... Juggernauting at high speed into oncoming traffic - tormented by a god-awful howlin' drunk driver and his hysterical sidekick, who laughing, whooped it up in one big ignite—jumping and hugging his seat as he looked through me with blanks that made panic take my heart and cause me to falter—screaming thoughts: 'We're all gonna fucking die!'

I've also been in the car of a serial killer. The first part of that metamorphic evening I spent roving the poorly lit back alleys of the town's cold-blooded underbelly with a HEAD gone on "Amarantium". And walking to my usual spot (on Dawnlit Drive) there I stood hitching a ride, when out from nowhere this suped-up machine pulled up—idling with a deep throaty gurgle.

And my first thoughts were: you gotta be fucking kidding

me—staring in disbelief as the car glowed like some hot rocket ship straight from the hurricanes of perdition... When suddenly, booting the passenger door open - the driver shouted: 'Bitch, you coming or what?!'

And already my cardiac valves were clapping like castanets during a hot-blooded gypsy dance duel - the driver revving that beast as I approached *VVROOM!* And just as I was about to enter the driver stabbed a large hunting knife into the passenger seat, growling: 'No fags!' And without hesitation I uttered my destination. And with mean bloodshot blues the driver stared me down and saw I wasn't gonna be any trouble. And ripping the knife out, placing it under his seat, he snarled: 'Okay.'

And so like a bitch on date night, I got in. But as I slammed the door shut - right then and there I knew I had cursed myself accepting that monster ride, as in a heartbeat, a shroud of malice envelope the car. The gurgling beast got kicked into gear and suddenly we were off like a shot—new dimension and all—the guy's face morphing—looking at me now with eyes of a shark: flat, no depth or feeling.

Then he pulled out something from his shirt pocket. His mind off the road as he stared at what appeared to be a photograph; proudly presented, to which my thoughts rang: concentrate on the goddamn road, you fuck. But he was delighted he had company, beaming at me all dumbstruck and gooey like a first-time dad showing off his newborn son - switching to gaze at the photo with a stupid grin, until, to my horror, I saw the image. At first I laughed. Thought it was some kinda sick joke. Then I realized this guy was for real. The snapshot was of a mutilated corpse. But only when he asked: 'So what do you think?' did I recognize the girl in the photograph. It was my friend, the adorable Saskia Amos—found one Wednesday morning stripped naked on the steps of the Methodist church in Auburn Hills. The killer had smashed her head repeatedly against the concrete. And then with a broken bottle cut her open.

A cold sickness swept over me.

Poor Saskia had had a crush on me—and I had butterfly feelings for her too. And once during a church/youth meeting; Friday night, she slipped me a love letter which I took with embarrassment. Her letter, reading: "Dear Freddy, Hi there! long time no see. So I hear that you like me. It was a big shock. I was talking to my pals when Erika came up to me and told me what you said. I always liked you, but I was too shy to tell you. I could never take my eyes off you. I am always looking at you. When I first came to this church, and I saw you, I already liked you. You are very nice looking. One thing is, whenever I try to get near to you, Shannon is always around you. Then I forget about talking to you. Well, there is not much to say but ... My ink is up, my pen is dry, but my love for you will never die. Love from Saskia ... Please write back." - I never did.

My friends teasing me as I took Saskia's letter. Her pudgy, dirty, unwashed hand the same moist hand she jerked older boys off with in the wino stairwells of Sweet Water Gardens: an impoverished block of ten three-storied flats. Saskia, young and in love with how much the boys lusted her chubby flesh. A girl with an angel heart - such a princess, who didn't deserve the short broken life that life dealt. Her sweat-stained sport pumps brushing the scattered burnt matches, cigarette stubs, and paper coils littering the narrow dark passages, as with the bad boys; their hands up her skirt and inside her panties, she slow-danced on a whirlwind of hormones and laughs—the burning will to express her poor trapped life through sex, alcohol and cigarettes, a rebel's freedom, a princess's right as she gave tongue and young-love—knocking empties over in the blunt jaded darkness... Sakia, with skirt swishing and hips swaying... Oh, how she loved to misbehave... Enthralled with her wild-blooded life - a torch that burnt like an altar of rebellion raised upon the highest of mountains... Her clammy skin always reeking tough of overcooked food, onions, sweat and nicotine. Saskia Amos, Age 15, a poor, ugly, unlucky girl—whose older brother Barry got sentenced for murder—stabbing his best friend in the heart during a drunken squabble. Both sat wired and blasted on the weathered steps of some rundown community flats. The hollow long corridors echoing with *cries* from hungry addict babies... When in a flash, deep emotions surfaced over an altercation the dead boy took to his grave. The only words before he died—crawling up the steps *to his flat* and into the arms of his girl and mother of his unborn child, was: "Barry did it..."

Ha-ha-ha! The killer let out a laugh that brought me back. I was in shock. The memory of Saskia, I remember... It was December 1990—when my mother broke the news. And for the whole night I sat sick and silent forever—and didn't come out my room for supper... Reading Saskia's letter over and over - unable to understand why she'd been taken in such a cruel heartless manner. They never caught the killer.

'She behaved badly, this one.' he sneered. I looked at the picture. It was exactly how the Māratopia Times described it. 5 December 1990 (The Wednesday Late Final): HEADLINE: 'Horror Movie' Murder: Girl's body found naked, mutilated. Crime reporter Wyatt Smith writing: 'The naked, mutilated body of a schoolgirl was found today outside a church in Auburn Hills after what has been described as a "horror movie" murder. Saskia Amos, 15, a Standard 6 pupil at Mountain View High was found in a pool of blood beside the Lighthouse Church in Kilgore Street at 1:30 am. Police said she had been attacked as she walked back to her home last night after visiting friends. Saskia's aunt, Mrs Estrella Chávez, said: "She was mutilated. Her body had been slashed from the groin to under her chin. "It was like a horror movie. Her face had been bludgeoned, and her eyes were protruding from her head. I could hardly recognise her."

The photograph of Saskia was dated with a felt tip pen: Dec 1990. When I saw this it made me swoon green with sickness. I whooshed.

'Hey whoa, easy there, buddy ... What's the matter, you don't like this one,' he chuckled—fanning himself with the Polaroid. 'I got even better ones. Here, this one I did two months ago ... A real piece of art, sliced her up nice and slow. I had so much fun. You know when you kill a certain part of the brain, you change the way the person interprets pain. Just a single blow to the head with a sharp pointed tool and she was turned into an attentive witness who chortled gurling blood while dying.'

'Wait...' I pined. The hard realization hitting me. For not only was this sick fuck getting kicks showing off his pastime pleasure: mutilating young girls... But soon he'd have to kill me too. Therefore, I had to make a break for it. But not helping my cause was the 'Amarantium' ... Now kicking into high gear.

All of a sudden my heart punched into clutch-burn and my chest tightened.

I grabbed my heart and gasped for air, unable to process the overflooding streaming-in of messages; a muddle-up of doubt and horror exhausting my brain, making it impossible to focus.

I closed my eyes but everything sped up hurtling larger, louder—similar to the overbearing rush one gets sucking on gasoline fumes... Your legs conk-in and your body twitches as if lassoed by an electric current, the sensation like that of hot gold coursing through your veins OR like being a kid again and playing on the yard tracks, clenching the rails... Feeling that current surge and make your muscles twitch - only the sensation of being blown on gasoline is 10x harsher, as closing your eyes, all you see are harsh thudding neons jelly fishing out there deep in the darkness beyond your lids.

I opened my eyes.

I was back in the car again. The interior bright and breathing as rivulets of mercury *now* began trickling down my spine. I shivered. Pale nausea whooshed through me and the car's interior began to spin. Hot and cold flushes shot through me - and my hands trembled. Suddenly my stomach burbled and I found I couldn't hold onto my dinner and retched all over the guy's arm. Over the wheel. The bright dazzling dash—EVERYTHING dripping in gastric juice and soggy food.

'Ooagg! You cunt! You fucking idiot, you serious? You fucking serious! Fuuck!? Fuk! Fuk! Fuk!' He bashed the steering wheel. 'Now you've done it...'

And with my hand in my coat pocket wrapped tightly around my axe, I was ready for anything.

And then he did it. He jabbed the accelerator; the engine making a guttural roar, and with a double-shot *BA-BANG!* we were off. That suped-up 1970 Chevy Chevelle SS swerving side-to-side and gunning like a beast on the loose along that long black stretch—passing cats eyes in one taillight streak. Yep "Serial killer and me"; a Happy Duo, locked into that fierce scream of metal and power as we hurtled downrange.

And then I sensed him itching for a kill. He was gonna go for it—looking all jumpy and agitated. And all he had to do was reach for that blade under his seat. As now with one hand on the wheel and the car firing along and bouncing, he went for the kill. But one-step ahead, I pulled out my axe in one swift motion and brought it down *K-RAKK!* smashing up his elbow. He shrilled like bitch and let go the wheel and in a panic tried pulling his arm out from under the seat—jerking it like mad to free himself and gain control as the car veered and dipped.

But before he could grab the wheel and jam on those breaks and bring our terror ride to a halt, I brought my axe down again *BASH!* This time smashing his knee, destroying it. His blood-curdling screams honey in my ears, as in that moment, looking at him: recalling his shark eyes once filled with power *but now* drooping with human tenderness, I wanted nothing more than to take his goddamn head off, as again *BAM!* I swung my axe, chopping his neck. Blood spurted everywhere, and with the arm I disabled, he tried applying pressure to the gaping wound in vain. 'That's for Saskia!' I hissed, spitting in his startled face as I bailed from the moving car. The impact from slamming into the blurry asphalt jarring the breath out of my lungs, as all I did was *just* lay there staring into the distance, watching, as the tail lights on that sleek brute-machine dissolved into the wet silvery darkness. And then all of a sudden the car slowed down and began to drift off the road, and with a bounce mounted the curb, the rear end jolting up as it smacked straight into the barrier with a loud *KRANG!*

In seeing this I sprang to my feet, a celebration cut short as instantaneously I balled up into a hunch. Intense pain gripping my body as staring at the killer's car I growled under my breathe: 'Yeah, take that you sonofabitch!'

I dragged myself off to a safe place to recover and assess what the fuck had just happend. But with sharp pains possessing every fiber in my body; deep breaths were impossible, leading me to surmise one of my lungs had collapsed, as then, finding a place in the shadows; tonguing chipped teeth, I spat grit and blood, my heart rolling in my aching chest as hunched over in a sweat, blinking and squinting from the saltiness that stung my eyes; sniffing perspiration off the end of my nose, I peered out from my hiding place to make sure the killer was dead for good.

4.

SAN COTTON

I got my good lift to drop me off at Sandina Lagoon on the outskirts of Saratoka Plains—where beneath palm trees swaying stretch-necked to a saturated sky, ready to burst showers, I strolled—listening to the muscular Pacific reverberate as it bruised the shores with heavy crashes that sucked back and sank into the smooth glittery sands with a fading hissle.

I passed Salsola Beach and the lighthouse and thought about the next day and bodyboarding - and if the morning surf report sounded promising - I'd ring up my good friend Léguvan Tiggs, the first person I ever took "Amarantium" with.

Thirty minutes before our participation as deacons in Holy Communion to commemorate the body and blood of the allegorical Saviour Jezem Jainko, Léguvan Tiggs and I, at Auburn Hills Seventh Seal Society Church, Māratopia, dropped Amarantium Viotriptamine for the very first time.

I first became intrigued by "amarant" thanks to the wild visual "trips" of my dynamic friend, San Cotton, who kept banging on in typing class about his momentous weekends *tripping* in vivid detail.

I met San Cotton in '92 at Backwood's Technical College: a refuge for dropouts concerned only with feeding their young minds and bodies with drugs, drink, sex, and every other fast thing young people love about life.

San and I hit it off immediately. A brother from another vagina, we both shared a sense of displacement in this ole world—along with a curiosity for mind-altering substances. But mostly it was San's rebellious streak that ignited something artistic and intellectual within.

From a young age—San Cotton's life had already turned bad—the day his alcky-dad came off the rails: unable to hold a job down—coming home each night drunk and mumbling under intoxication—harboring a grievance or two that he wished he'd put to his manager (face-to-face) only to end up arguing with their dent-ridden fridge—punching it each night and making such a racket the neighbors thought a madman lived next door. His wayward spiral fracturing their family through his love for booze and a contempt for authority. But one day his wish came true. He tried to settle the score by taking a clumsy inaccurate swing at his manager's head, only to miss out right and fall over. And even though the punch had missed its mark, the attempted assault was enough to give San's dad the sack. And so feeling sorry for himself and drinking to feel better, but only feeling worse—San's dad got caught up in an alcoholic circle of self-punishment and self-redemption. But without the self-drive to look for another job in order to keep his family together—they lost it all: the house, car, the possessions; even their beloved pets: a brown Boxer and a white kitten had to be terminated. But what was even sadder was San Cotton's mom: always wearing that dirty pink gown *of hers* with cigarette and stove burns. A lovely lazy lady with a face beaten by booze—who shared her husband's thirst for the demon drink. And so when that blackened day came: the wolf arrived at their door and blew their nice little family apart, forcing San, his older brother, and kid sister to fend for themselves. Their adolescence spent in and out of boarding homes and rough schools—that by the time I met San, he was eagle smart and streetwise with a cynical twist. The emotional scars of paternal backhanders and depression from an early age already having cemented a *restlessness* within: "sufferings-a-brewin'"—along with secret ticking bombs and psychological setbacks. San (age-17) already on file at the Psycho Unit at Māratopia County Hospital on the slopes of Lime Rock Peak—Ward G22.

And with his 1950s rebel-cool good looks and carefree

charm—San Cotton became popular amongst the nurses. They loved him. "The danger" of a life on the edge... His romantic puzzling attempts at suicide, and record near deaths - "The whole package", sparking a maternal warmth within these ladies of the ward. San Cotton, after all, unwittingly having compiled an almanac of "Trouble". A list that included: slashed arms, self-inflicted accidents, episodes of overdose, and bouts of self-poisoning: such as the legendary Insecticide Incident. A feat he achieved downing half a glass of Thornback bug juice. A genuine guinea pig death dare, that would've had any super cockroach twitch like an amateur. And bless the angels that are placed among us. For if it wasn't for San Cotton's steadfast sister, Lissa Cotton, who rushed him to Emergency to have his stomach pumped after finding him on the kitchen linoleum turning purple and frothing; busy with his (own) death, I would not have been blessed with San Cotton.

5.

BERTHA TEXIROSA

AND San Cotton fell on a bad year after finding his dear buddy, the tender-hearted Elias, parked in the garage; a Methadexotrine pipe in hand, DEAD by carbon-monoxide suicide. The guy only 26. We all used to go surfing together, smoke weed, and explore ourselves on "Xycamorphinol" during them long hot summers of '96 & '97. Besides, the guy had everything. Good "turbo" looks, a hot girl, good job, a car, studying to be a veterinarian... But one day a supernatural experience on both Amarantium and Xycamorphinol (Ether)—or what is called a 'scudflip'—spooked the bejezem out of him. His bedside lamp started talking, and as a result, poor Elias developed an *itch-up* on the brain. Cos after that 'High' he never got so high. And made a bad turn, hooked on Methadexotrine or "Flashbang" (a highly addictive stimulant). Explaining that the Flashbang-high or 'cracked-eye' as he labelled it—was like having a huge tongue lick his brain out. Excusing this habit as the only way to lick-calm whatever intense parasite was eating away at his mind—making him go all *fucked-up* insane.

And so it was to be this love-of-a-drug that pile-drove poor Elias' soul. Elias, at first, pawning his stereo, then pinching his mama's purse, and later on his old man's TV. His old man left staring into an empty corner of adapters and cables - wondering what had become of his once beloved son. And soon Elias lost his job, quit his studies, and walked out on his girl... All for the love of a cracked-eye - throwing his soul out with the rags - doing himself wrong... Falling deep into a depressive state; until that fateful day, when gunning that pedal he filled his lungs - licking that insect to soothe his brain—doing himself in. That "devil's dirt" taking him along on a one-way ticket ride to the Land of Great Escapes. Yep. Poor ole Elias. A young man with a good soul who turned his back on this ole Town of Pain for good.

And so after that things spiraled badly for San in a real unlucky way. Like the night I carried him to Emergency to get stitches. Both of us slaughtered on alcohol, weed, and pills. San spinning round on a barstool as if the world couldn't get any better... But slipping off he cut the tendons in his hand on the very beer bottle he had been whistling a sailor shanty into. The tune of his demise: "The Bonny Ship The Diamond". And after that night San couldn't play guitar like he used to... Recalling them times in his stale candlelit room: stretched out on wooden floorboards all stared up at the nicotine-coated ceiling, smoking weed; the most chilled-out time of my life, as listening and floatin' in a dream; all in love with my friendship with San, I'd close my eyes and smile as my man picked a handful of wistful tunes... My favorite being: "Is There Anybody Out There" by Pink Floyd.

And after months in rotten bandages, San's hand healed wrong. A deep scar making it impossible for his pinky and ring finger to hold the chords. And when he tried, I died. For that carefree heart I always knew as San was filled now with nothing but tears. Tears that slid down his cheek and into his mouth, causing him to gulp heartsore sorrow... For with no tunes to put PEACE into San's restless soul, it killed my man. My once happy friend growing sadder by the day... Capable only of strumming a dull drone. His attempts at lifting himself as pathetic as watching a sad bird with a snapped wing flapping in vain, trying to reach the prize in the sky. And in his struggle, San almost gave up. Lamenting how he wanted a hole in the ground beside ole Elias. And all I could do to distract my poor good friend from suiciding himself, was to spend more time by his side.

And as such, the death of Elias and all other kinds of karmic woes caught up and poisoned San. And one day he woke up with a boil the size of a squash ball; back of his neck, and had to have it lanced at the sick house. The doctor with a scalpel puncturing it... And then, making a small incision, squeezed out all the pus and juice, sewing it back up. And with that fresh wound suppurating and needing to be swabbed with tonic several times a day... Making tea for both of us... While San had his back toward me... Instead of nursing my inflicted friend - I pressed a boiling hot teaspoon to that raised little wound (back of his neck)—looking as it like a moist open gash. And shrieking in pain, San got so mad, he tugged off my green corduroy flat cap I'd been fashioning at the time; going through my unsuccessful shaven-headed gay-monk trials. And throwing it in the toilet, he pissed on it. And I demanded to know why he peed on my cap. And he told me I behaved like a cruel prick.

And for the whole day, as a result of the "teaspoon burning incident"... After a great momentous morn making and eating breakfast together like a snug couple... Along with trying to wipe a neon stain *that didn't exist* off my grandparents' vinyl countertop; house-sitting their sweet little home for a week; laughing under hallucinations on "THC-butter", we never spoke for the whole 'high' - avoiding one another; being too paranoid - for I feared San was hatching plans against my bones *with shovels in his eyes;* ready to bury me in the backyard, having overheard him sat in the next room *with* curtains drawn, twiddling thumbs and muttering mojos in the dark. And on this particular day - in fact for the whole week - something weird hung over us. Something for which we already had a name. We called it "The Rakashaan". And whenever San and I went too far "The Rakashaan" would emerge. And then soon enough, objects would begin flying across the room or time would freeze. It was quite a heavy thing we conjured. Not to be taken lightly.

After our comedown, it emerged that San had heard the same ramblings emanating from me - hidden squeezed in the kitchen cupboard beneath the sink. Both of us for most of that week like sad unconscious boys—dealing with our own blind delight - brains creaking beneath the heaviness of our stoney trial - poisoned by dread and mind-altering perceptions of self.

And so like this San and I had many strange times together. All of them mad missions. LIFE stole from the depths beyond the stone set night. Recalling one unforgettable beaut, an incident we called: The Gatecrash Party:

She was big, beautiful and fancied me - and as I massaged her feet, I made her skinny boyfriend with proud-arm around his "baby whale", jealous.

It began on a Friday night at Champs: a pool hall out in Flagston. San and I already SNARLED on a mixture of booze, Bioplus (energy tonic), painkillers, and weed. When bumping into an old friend - the adorable Bertha Texirosa that at the time was with on-and-off boyfriend Lefty—who we both invited to join our table.

And soon enough, as anticipated, Lefty stormed off over my constant advances toward his 'Black Diamond'. Bertha relishing the attention. Using me to make Lefty rage sweet jealousies— hoping that one day he'd discover that connection between mind, heart, and balls—that place *pure* where beauty and destiny merge into one true sweet deep dive at chance.

And to stop the evening from souring—Bertha announced it was her birthday. And ever the sucker-gent, San suggested a party back at his pad: a rented house shared with his sister Lissa and Tiffany, his pregnant ex: who for free highs got banged-up by the town's top "Xycamorphinol" dealer. The selfsame prick San and his ex-convict cousin Marky: a toothless prison-bitch, covered head-to-toe in gang tattoos, would sometimes smoke Diamorphix with after a long night raving on "Ether", Proloxytin, and pills.

And the timing couldn't have been better - the house empty for at least several hours. Lissa and Tiffany, both bare naked dancers, shakin' chicken 'n' ass down at some sleazy bar in the shit-stick end of town; right up until the cracklings of dawn.

And Bertha couldn't contain herself—flapping her hands and holding them to her face as she screamed. After which, cheekily, she asked San if a few of her friends could come over. And gallantly naive, San agreed:

'Yeah, no problem, bring 'em along, we'll have a real smokin' time.'

And thrilled, Bertha reached over, spilling her tits as she grabbed San, burying his face in her buttery cleavage—stroking his head, cooing: 'That's my, boy.'

But San pulled away, blushing shy fury, embarrassed as he fixed himself, thinking: was she mad? Bertha (all the while) giving San a fond look, while cackling a playful smile.

Back at San's pad now, the three of us danced to SUN FM's party hour—swilling back Magma Coolship's in the high summer heat of '95. Attitudes a-changing now. This afterall "a new Māratopia". Young, positive, hopeful, free, alive, and yes—colorful. For this was world where legends roam, goddamnit! Nothing could befall us, when suddenly, three loud bangs rattled the front door. Wary as a cat with a flea in its jacket, we all looked to one another, sensing something deliberate had rocked-up to spoil our good fun.

And being MAN of the house—with a handsome swagger that told you he was in charge; his hairy chest in full bloom—dressed in torn jeans, white trunks, worn-in lumberjacks—a beer bottle in hand—pouting a 7-Clouds ciggie, with head tilted back; San opened up. And right then and there, drop-jawed—his cig fell sparks to the floor. His face saying it all: un-fucking-believable - as there in front of him - stood a pickup load of *genuine excitement* ready to cast their bones onto the fire of good times - all of 'em reeking of weed and shouldering crates of home brewed supplies: mezcal and Pisco - enough overproof artillary to carpet bomb a small village of brain cells, as now the lot of 'em, laughing, stood animated - making a big scene; loud and uncouth, going nowhere.

Suddenly Bertha ran over, clapping madly—them giggly tits of hers, bouncing, as she bumped San outta the way *who flew* into the wall (his good heart bruised), Bertha's bovine-mass engulfing the doorway, as tongue-in-cheek; pretending to be "lady of the house", she welcomed her friends.

And with shoulders slumped, San sipped his beer bitterly—looking all shot-eyed and dejected - staring at the floor and thinking: this could go either of two ways: fucked or fucked-up.

After 30 min, though—all TENSIONS melted into the ether and the party got underway. Spirits boosted by the extra booze. As everyone now down on the worn living room carpet danced in a tight little group of sweat and smiles, smoke and mirth. Ages ranging 20 to 50. And no sooner were San and I flying high in fun—when another barrage of loud BANGS shook the front door. This time though: San and I, in the kitchen; not around to answer—were caught paying mind and money to some slutty girl—"Five buckskins a-look" - a sexy little thang, who touted her pussy, as the two of us like punters at the races, cheered her on, as she lifted her skirt and pulled away her panties—showing us her rough stuff.

And by now the door had long been answered. A further two packed pickup loads spilling into the house straight from the county's wild side out in Bendablo Hills. This new mob more threatening and morose than the first bunch.

And I guess it musta been "All The News"—spread round the squat-fires - little whispers buzzin' of a "House party that was gonna get smashed" - Hot-gossip equal to a street banner advertising: FREE STUFF, GRAB ALL YOU CAN.

And so like a band of coyotes drawn to injured prey, this ragged outfit overran the house like a raiding party looking to pillage supplies and pilfer valuables. And as a result, worst thoughts of death came to mind. For in our state we would've been easy kill. Cos I know blokes from the Sierras. Worked with them one summer laying pipes and digging trenches - filling wheelbarrows - carting mound loads along narrow ledges with ease. Firm as woodcutters these blokes - built like shaven, oiled-down stallions. One smack and they'll rock your skull like a bell. Your brains leaking out your ears like raspberry snot.

'Bro, if these fucking dudes jump us, we got no chance.' I told San.

'Yeah, tell me about it, that dude with a lazy eye … He's been clocking me out the whole night … That dead-eye just sitting there like a mad Mona Lisa on a cheap 'high'. Goddamn it! Who invited that prick.' sniffed San.

The guy with the lazy eye was a notorious killer who ran by the nickname Madero.

'Fuck, bro, what do we do?'

'Just play it like you mean it, don't keep checking him out … That fool is a damn animal … Served seven for bludgeoning a guy to death; charged-up on paraffin-wine and pills. Bashed the guy's skull in with a claw hammer. Then for a laugh pissed in his skull like it was a pisspot. And all the guy did was ask him for the time.'

'Yeah, well, there ain't no time.'

'Psh, yeah, I bet he knows that now. That incident taking place way before Madero developed that bad eye, though.' noted San.

'You mean at one point he actually looked normal?'

'Huh! That fucker went into prison with eyes of steel, only to come out with one eye pooped.'

'Fuckin' jokes, right.'

'Tsss, yeah. Heard they dug him out so badly in there, he snapped a brain vessel and ended up talking with a goddamn stammer. They ripped the asshole out of that poor bastard. The damage was so severe that in the beginning stages of his collapse he was like a fucking baby. Had to be taught the basics all over again. How to feed himself. Wipe his own ass; even how to piss straight.'

'Sonofabitch.'

'Yeah. Then after about two years in a home for crazies they released him back into society, just like that.'

'Jeez, what were they thinking?'

'Yeah, well, that's just it - they don't. Just remember, the system relies on a certain amount of crazy and fucked-up to flow back into its pastures. It's the way they maintain the balance. Keeping the lions amongst the lambs, you know.'

'Hmm? I wonder where our friend Mr Extreme Eye-Contact over there fits in.'

'Yeah, well, he don't. At least a wild animal has fucking integrity. But with this guy, he has no moral compass. A guy like that can never fit into society - it's just now he's wired.'

'Survival mode at it's most pure.'

'Fucking pure delinquency more like it. Creative mode turned off; no intelligence - just one hundred percent darkside fear and ego, maan. I mean, just look at the fucker. The only thing stopping him right now from jumping up and ripping my face off are probably the meds his dosed-up on. Pray that shit don't wear off - cos the only wild animal that's safe is a tranqued one. The guy's on a range of pills. Pain prescription. Antidepressants, you name it. I'm always seeing him down at Ward G22 trying to get more than his prescription will allow - always harassing the staff like it's his fucking right to be a mean asshole. And no one does a fucking thing. Appears everyone just makes an effort to look the other way.'

'Yeah, well, just look at him - he's ate up about something, alright. Bastid looks crazier than a shit-house rat.'

And so without a clear plan on how to get everyone out the house, and both a little tense, we ended up taking our frustration out on one another.

'Goddamnit, man - why'd Bertha bring so many people ... Lissa's gonna have a fit when she gets home.'

'You suggested the party. And to be fair ... I think Bertha only invited a handful.'

'Yeah, well, whichever way, I'm screwed. The time is already 1 am. Fuck!'

This tricky little incident now promised to be the bring-down of this lovely Dutch gable—landlorded by a crazy ass crackasoid named Karol, who did everything in heroic doses, as each night he'd have his asshole opened up like a can of worms—screeching out back in the dank, stale, guest quarters: wet with smells of kitten faeces and mildew. Karol, whose sodomite howls could be heard as far as the rail tracks. Intense thrusts on his prostate with mouth agape—whimpering: 'Sweet Jezem!' as hot semen shot up his ass while he and boyfriend "Rectum Ranger" Declan: a deaf-mute with a stump foot; lit up like fiends on a smorgasbord of drugs, emptied their souls through anal sex in the dirty carnalistic night, blistered on spirits and weed, pills and Proloxytin - caked in their own effluent, butt jam, and semen like natives of some lost sacred mud tribe. Karol screaming 'Ruby! Oh sweet Ruby!' to the sinews of this world's rocking bones. Ruby, the pet name Karol gave Declan's glowing orifice for obvious bloody reasons, as Declan's poor sphincter; all used-up from the constant pumps, never had time to heal - therefore was always in a state of scabbing over or being ripped up raw.

And one time after a grueling session of anal bombardment and cock-gagging—Karol barraged into the house head-to-toe in shit; a glass of premium potty-water brandy raised, as crack-voiced he shrieked: "Crowned in spin fire with velvet leviathan desires, beast seraphim spellbound surround, like cold flaming vampires!" And with that, Karol froze, eeked and timbered over landing face first.

I looked at Bertha now, who looked pretty delicious, screaming inside to poke her in the ole whiskers. And so after a few more joints and woody spirits to stoke up the sex drive, to my delight, my dream got answered: Bertha and I striken *somehow* dumbly in love. Two flames burning in the night. My hormones lit as I buzzed an itch for that soft, warm salmon-hole.

And so playing it cool, I curtailed my moves into a Class-A act. Bertha's pheromones HUMMING like a chorus of sweet cicadas as whispering sexual monotones in her ear, I sucked her lobe, hooking her delights, making her giggle and shy away. And then for a second she fell serious, looking at me with that longing look all girls give when they imagine a boy to be theirs. Bertha giving the game away with a loving smile. And right then I knew I had been granted access to her palace. The both of us slipping away for a quickie.

Flumping onto her back, Bertha slid her big-girl panties down shiny shins and over chipped toes nails. The scent of her dripping muff hittiing my core—putting a stitch in my heart; along with a breathlessness that made me salivate, as crossing my heart and hoping to die—I plunged in like any good man with a love for life and its precious moments.

Lifting Bertha's woollen jersey—I pulled away her floral bra cup and began nibbling on big erect berries. My hairy ballsack slapping against her blue steak petals, as Bertha, darting her tongue in and out of my mouth, tightened her thighs around my waist. My thrustage now deep-end, to the point I wanted to climb right up inside her pussy all way down to the wrought iron soul of Momma Gaia, as now bleeding out sweet emotion, I shed a dry tear in my cool effort. Strong on the job, my love-work in driblets of sweat began beading up, sizzling off my buttocks and rolling in drips onto the carpet like melted butter.

Locked in and going at it strong: a solid *five minutes* of dumb pumping, like champs of "cosmic love"—with foreheads pressed together—Bertha and I, in tearful groans of sweet union charged rhythmically—until all of a sudden—DAYLIGHT—Bertha's eyes widened as she pulled a face and cacked a moan—to which I answered back—popping my buttermilk seed inside her hot guts—'Oooaah!'

Sneaking back to the party, I did up my jeans, and Bertha

ran her hand down her inner thigh—for her pants to soak up my semen trickling from her soggy vagina.

We joined the party and noticed there was plenty of food for everyone. All the guests slobbering and sucking greasy animal flesh and licking fingers; smacking lips—crunching animal carcasses in the form of steak, thighs, chops, ribs, sausage, you name it.

'What's all this crap, then?' I observed
And Bertha, the birthday girl, not saying a word - cheered happily—embracing San, saying: 'Oh, San, this is by far the best birthday bash I've ever had ... I don't know how to thank you.' Bertha, once again ready to bury San's face in her sticky cleavage. But San pulled away... Nostrils flared. Lips pursed. He was vexed - all cross-armed as he hawk-eyed everyone with suspicion. Holding doubts as to the origin of the meat.
Suddenly someone cranked up the music. The house now rammed elbow-to-elbow like a saloon hall filled thick with riot and revelry. Some of the guys and girls groping one another—danced in groovy little hugs. Some swayed solo. Others in groups cracked rapacious jokes, while a few voicing deep-seated resentment; along with political views, preached in booze-fuelled outburst. San exclaiming: 'Fuck this shit, talk about the darkest winter of the soul. I mean, literally, there is no fucking way I am going to get all these fuckers to leave before Lissa gets home.' It was horrendous alright. The situation was fucked. They were just slowly wrecking the place, spilling their drinks and leaving stains everywhere—walking bits of meat and fat into the rug—streaking food across the linoleum. Their greasy fingers smearing the light switches, doorknobs, the white surfaces and tiles. Even the fridge door, and counter tops, the walls— EVERYTHING marked up in gunky hand and fingerprints.

Meanwhile, in the lounge doorway—caught up in our own little love scene—Bertha and I stood oblivious to it all, as I sucked and ate bits of meat off the tip of her tongue (in them days when I was still a vile carcass eater)—squeezing her tasty butt.

Then there was a flare-up. Aggressive accusations and objections. Shit got real. There was a scuffle and then I heard San holding a shouting contest with several of the unwelcomed guests in the kitchen.

It turned out the meat didn't belong to any of the guests. Everyone, except San, ended up eating the meat that belonged to the members of the household. And when San found out, boy was he pissed. The bastids had raided the freezer and had cooked up an entire two month's supply of meat in a large electric frying pan. But not only that. The evening had turned into a free-for-all. EVERYONE helping themselves to WHATEVER. Drawers, cupboards, lids left open. Utter pandemonium. One character was even caught spooning down chock-fulls of cooked spaghetti from a torn tin can. While several others stood around the electric frying pan dipping and scooping up fat and grizzle with hunks of bread which they ate like cake. They were having an absolute gem of a time.

Then San clocked one guy slipping the household's toaster under his jacket. The guy just about ready to make a duck for it, when: 'Hey, fuck-turd!' called San. And the guy would have made a clean break; if it wasn't for San's reflexes, who, lunging forward, grabbed the guy by the collar—yanking it so hard the guy spun into an awkward little twist that sent the toaster flying one-way (smashed to bits) while the guy *CRACK!* smacked his pip against the floor.

And San, leaning over the guy, eyeballed him, pointing to what was left of the toaster, going: 'A cold crumpet don't melt butter, bitch!'

And dazed, the guy drew a fearful: 'Huh?' Shaking his groggy head. But in no time he was up on his feet again; wobbling like a punch-drunk sailor, who, bolting for the front door, got helped-on by San who gave him a firm boot to the coccyx, cursing: 'Taste leather up your ass, you bastid!' The momentum from the kick sending the guy off course *SMACK!* face first into the door post. And again the guy was down, but once more got up like a champion of tough licks - scrambling through the front door free and luckily escaping another flying boot as he shot out the house and down the street in a hot pelt—shouting: ''Touch down!' loud enough the entire street could hear. His arms stretched out like a glider. Such out of place behavior. Although a week later—with San needing buckskins from his secret piggy bank for the purpose of scoring a brick of Arango weed, five tabs of "Amarant", a carton of 7-Clouds, and several bottles of El Scuffo wine for another grand weekend of highs-and-whys (on the menu of how to get proper WRECK-TUMED)—San found no money. Then he clocked on—recalling the toaster thief and his out of place behavior; celebrating down the road *like that* after getting his ass rumpled. The guy well over the moon, having stolen the amount equivalent to three weeks wages. San's humble barman work: listening to the tall tales of losers and unloved women, amounting to fuck all.

San walked over to the stereo and flipped the music off, announcing:

'Alright you fuckwads, that's it—party over. You can all piss off now!'

And just like that the atmosphere splooshed to the floor.

Suddenly protest filled the air. Chaos and ANGER. Nobody wanted to leave. So nonchalantly, doing what any solemn dude would do in times of strife, San lit a smoke and went over to the fridge (in the hope of grabbing a manly ice old beer), but to his grief, found only a jar of pickling juice and a shriveled up carrot. The fuckers had raided the fridge, picking it clean to the bone.

'Bro.' I said, concerned—giving an empathetic eye to eye. But San blanked me, already inflicted with a look of abandon as he brushed by. When just then, someone stepped in his way.

It was Madero.

'You just fucked up, chief, cos if you think I am driving all the way back to Bendablo Hills, you got another thing coming. I'm sleeping here tonight. In fact I'm taking your bed, along with your bitch's ass.' And San, looking at Madero, dropped his shoulders—and with a sigh, shook his head—uttering a defeated: 'So it's gonna be like that, huh?'

But after only a few seconds... Being the stubborn, hard-headed fool that San was, he raised his head, thumbed his crooked nose, and squared up to Madero—staring at him straight-eyed, going: 'I don't know. I really don't know about that. My bed is my bed, and the girl I once had, well she been bred-up by some next man: another fucking low IQ just like you, bitch. So look here, I tell you what, you can sit on this finger (San flippng Madero "the bird") cos what you want, ain't ever gonna manifest, motherfucker. You rocked-up here uninvited; all gung-ho and shit, thinking to drive this house into the ground. But the party is over, maan—so just take every uninvited, freeloader motherfucker with you aboard that shit bucket you call a ride, and fuck off!'

Madero, loving the interaction, going: 'Oh, she's got some bite in her. Bit of a phenomenon, aintcha.' San looking at Madero thinking: what the fuck you on about, maan. Madero, juiced up now, continuing: 'First time in the history of this world, that a dead man gets to sign his own death certificate, ha ha ha ha.' Madero's mad eye popping out. Yep, you just made a fatal error, chief, don't know who you fucking with?!'

'Actually, yeah, I do. Heard all the colorful stories. You even made a name for yourself, they called you the "Joint", on account of you being passed around so much like the communal bitch - why you were being cream pied everyday on that prison block, weren't you?'

'What?!' Madero's face dropping in disbelief. Silence falling like an Autumn mist.

'Yeah, my cousin Marky, a prison bitch like you, served in the same prison. He got to know all the juicy details. Them guys took a real fancy to you, didn't they. Heard they were balls deep inside your ass every motherfucking day; digging you out. Pure animals, just runnin' a train on your ass ... filling you up like a slush bucket. Yeah, I know pretty much all there is to know about you.'

And at the mention of his past, Madero turned into a contemplative, philosophical man of deep ruminations. Undertones of regret and nightmarish hells undulating as he spoke with a stammer.

'Hmmm. Fair enough. Yeah, I did walk that line. I bore that cross. And belieeeve me, you don't want to know what's at the bottom of that pit. I'm talking unspeakable sorrow and dispair. But at the end of it, I gained a clarity; you just never know until you know. I mean, it's built into every creature to want to live, yes? Somehow there's always that flicker of hope. But in prison, doing hard time, all you want is to fucking die. Dark memories, maan. They fucking raped me so much in there - up to twenty times a day for seven years. And as a result, I completely lost myself. They fucking broke my spirit, man. Hardcore pumps so intense and fuelled with so much rage, that my one eye; unable to take the constant pressure, got afflicted. That's how I ended up with this "Pooped-eye", along with a stammer. Those sick fucks turned me into a goddamn Picasso. And as a result, I can't even have a heart-to-heart with anyone. Have you ever addressed somebody, only to have them look around, wondering who the fuck you're talking to? (San looking around, caught himself, though too late) Tct! You see, even you are a sell out piece of shit (Madero shaking his head) Fuck! I fucking hate people, maan. The humiliation I have to go through every day, it's fucking tedious (Madero giving San a distrustful, but thoughtful look) I can't even get pussy without having to pay for it nowadays. It's like wherever I turn, there is always some useless piece of shit that is gonna fuck up my day. People going so far as to actually toy with my disability. Granted, you might expect a slip of concentration from some random person, but not a professional, right. And a prostitue, now that's a fucking professional. I'm paying for your service, so in respect of the transaction, it never should become personal. But they are no different. Just the same as everyone else - all shy and on edge, wanting to avoid the eye contact, you know, unsure of my ability to return it. One stupid bitch even yelled out aloud; making a big scene and all, saying that it freaked her out. I mean, fuck! Can you imagine that. So here I am, man-to-man—asking you, straight up—can you honestly look me in the eye, and take me seriously?'

And for what it was worth, San tried keeping the moment real - concentrating real hard on Madero's good eye. But like a convergent point, he got drawn to the lazy one. And unable to help himself, he totally lost it, blurting out exactly what was on everybody else's mind, going: 'Oh, for fucksakes, maan! Why don't you just slap an eyepatch on it and retire that fucker!'

Oh man, here we go, I thought. Whaaat in fuck's name? I'm looking at a dead man here.

And just then Madero pulled out a huge hunting knife—causing everyone in the room to draw their breath. And with my hand in my jacket pocket, wrapped around my axe handle, I knew I would be only escalating an already tenuous situation if I threw my axe into the mix.

Madero bore down on San, going: 'Uh-uh, I don't think so, chief. No one, and I mean no one, insults THE EYE.' scowled Madero who all of a sudden stabbed the knife—JAH!—7-inches of Damascus steel missing San by millimeters. Madero screaming: 'I'll finish you!' Going mad as he moved all over and around San—exclaiming: 'I'll stick you here! Stick you here!'—stabbing over San's heart, his stomach, 'Stick you here!'—between the ribs: piercing a lung, 'Stick you here!'—going around—behind the earlobe 'Stick you here!'—finding a nice opening: 'Stick you here!' spiking a kidney—and coming back round in a crouching position slashing San's groin area: his thigh: the femoral. Madero moving like a trained killer, making-out, each time with force, to stab or slash San with a mortal blow—as he repeated his killing mantra: 'Stick you here! Stick you here! Stick you here!'—going under San's chin: slitting the jugular—and then stab, stab - taking the eyes out. Madero lunging with such strength, speed and control that the power behind each feigned-strike made San's heart skip huge beats, as stood frozen, his mind raced off dizzily. And swallowing hard with eyes closed San offered a whisper: a prayer, as standing his ground and swaying with a complexion white as a sail, San awaited death's ship to spirit him home.

Then all of a sudden Madero stopped. Complete silence. Everyone in the room awaiting the killer touch.

San quivered. But noticing *the hush* in the room—fearfully opened his eyes.

'Ha! I bet you shat yourself, huh? Next time you play me for a pussy-ass, you won't be so lucky, chief. I'll finish you and stuff you back up your mother's vagina, piece-by-piece. Then, I'll slit her throat (motioning with his thumb) and drain her out and drink her blood like gravy, you get me?'

And San, not knowing what to do, stood pegged to the spot with a glazed deer-like stare, looking at Madero as if he was the death dealer himself.

And none of us wanted to die that night, but someone would.

'What you think you doing, huh, eyeballing me like that, you trying to grow a pair or something? Madero, pushing his mug right up into San's grill now.

Oh, shit biscuits, I thought. What prompted San to go into full-on stare-out mode. He must have been wishing his own exit. My heart (at this point) racing like a hamster having a panic-shit. The whole situation tenuous like some hot new saga of excessive indulgences, partying, sex, brawlings and confession—all spiraling toward some bold tragic climax. My hand now tighetning around my axe handle—pitting me against the decision to kill or be calm. WHEN suddenly, the boldest, yet dumbest thing ever: Bertha for some reason jumped between San and Madero. But soon enough, when logic caught up with emotion, Bertha realized her error - stood now in the face of danger. And then she saw it: the animal in Madero's eye. And realizing she did not want to die that night—she began trembling - welling-up - worried for her life, as she broke into tears—splashing rivers of insult all over Madero's hard, mean face... Cussing him-out for making her feel so vulnerable. The stress of the moment causing Madero's mad eye to twitch. For *at once* I saw the true derangement of Madero. His soul bottling rage an indication he was on the verge of doing something real bad—as smiling at Bertha, Madero winked. And in that precise moment, I saw the killer in his eye. Madero's premeditative-smirk holding only one thing in mind: to kill Bertha. And right then, I made up my mind that I was gonna kill Madero. But luckily, I wasn't the only one in the room who saw the telegraphed message. Cos without warning, before I had time to whip out my axe and bash Madero's temple *WHAMMO!* like a bolt, Madero got bitched... Drooling on the carpet like a party pooper. And so this was to be the undoing of Madero. A brick-fist square to the jawbone cancelling his killer agenda and straightening his mad-eye (for just a millisecond) piling him to the floor, while rocking his brains out.

    And as he lay there, eyes open, Madero appeared quite normal; handsome in fact. But gradually as that lazy eye fell back out of alignment, Madero, once again, appeared mad.

    'Lefty!' Exclaimed Bertha, 'My Lefty, you saved me.' embracing and kissing him.

And just in time, Lefty must have caught drift of the gatecrash—hanging round the weed shacks and oil drum braziers of twilight with a quart of beer in hand and a heartbreak joint for company; staring into the flames—stewing jealousies over my buttering-up of his beloved, when luckily in ear-shot, Lefty caught the faded ends of BROADCAST that made known of a house party in Flagston; thrown as a birthday gift for a girl by the name of Bertha, that was gonna get proper smashed. And in hearing this, Lefty jumped up and throttled the two drunkards—interrogating their boastings and sozzled visions of loot in the night. Ramblings about how a fancy suburban abode was gonna get sunk. Their mumblings enough to draw sense though, and draft Lefty for his love.

And so now it was Lefty who stood and shone chest-out radiant. A real man. His one foot on Madero who lay slain.

Lefty had finally staked his claim. Bertha all over him like a wet puppy. Her heart: a knee-trembling gush of breathless emotion. She wanted his dick deep—kissing and hugging him—wanting nothing but to suck all his juices out. And as for me, I was relegated to being just another soggy foray between Bertha's rubbery thighs. For it was Lefty now who transpired as her Man of the Year. For not only did Lefty curb Bertha from getting brutally stabbed, but he also prevented San's jugular from jetting out all over the living room carpet.

Lefty took charge and we thanked him. He was even cool with me. His biting conflict, I guess, having put things into a broader view—making him see just how Bertha made him feel; having fallen crazy-psycho for that girl. And so with one gallant act Lefty became Bertha's shining steed. His ballsack bubbling babies - his cock crowing hard - his heart standing true - mind focused - for he saw a future *at last*—a happy man he was; his sperm having finally found a home.

Others jubilantly helped carry Madero out the house—

throwing him into his own beat-up pickup that now got proudly driven off by its new owner.

Lefty loaded up his brother's pickup the "steed-machine" that helped him in his "race over" to save-the-day—cramming in as many people as possible. As then slamming the doors, Lefty sped off with Bertha sat beside hugging his arm. The pair of 'em like a bunch of love-struck dizzy fools.

And after that interlude of chance I never saw Bertha or her blue steak petals ever again.

Later on I caught rumour that Madero got turfed into a roadside gully. His corpse lying among old tires, paint cans, and rubble. Apparently he never woke up. In fact the moment Lefty laid that blow and rocked his skull—Madero was already walking with his ancestors.

It was a night of death and love. A night that those who were there will never forget, as consequently, straight into bed Lefty took his prize. My iridescent semen still caked down Bertha's inner thighs like snail spit, as Lefty—peeling open Bertha's fat juicy toad pumped it all night long and into the mists of dawn—unloading his genetic junk deep inside her cold porridge pot. And when Bertha gave birth. Everyone said the babba had my eyes.

6.

LÉGUVAN TIGGS

REVELING in San Cotton's colorful reveries on "amarant"—and how "a beauty of untamed variety" unlocked his genuine self—Léguvan Tiggs, after I revealed all forms of San "Piper" Cotton's holy dream, was in need of no further convincing. The subject of dropping 'amarant' as exciting as tales of finding hidden treasures of gold and gems.

A kindred spirit and fellow mind of fire—Léguvan and I were inseparable, as most of our "first-time experiences" we fire-walked together.

Both brainwashed and immersed into the Seventh Seal Society Church system, Léguvan and I were its hopeful protégés, programmed and crowned chosen well before our minds were set, all groomed-up to one day carry the torch of doctrine *perilously* into the world - unknowningly doomed with the seed of dogma implanted as deep as psychosis runs cold. We also attended the same school run by the same freakish-cult - ALL hard-edged followers of the creepy Brekem Young, founder and leader of the Seventh Seal Society Church; out in the ominous vicinity of Auburn Hills.
And both Léguvan and I lived in Sweet Place village where in Peaceful Meadow Park, smoking our first cigs, we fell horribly ill. Dead Leaf's I recall—inhaled on a windy day. And we didn't get home until three hours later, missing supper that night, sat green on the park bench - wondering why we lit up at all.
And going back a few years now... In the boys cloakroom;

secondary school—we skipped class to sip awful shots of rag water *that* Léguvan pinched from his daddy's tumble-down bar: a hastily knocked-up chipboard creation erected in their living room. Léguvan's dad: the legendary Davy 'Deuce'—keeping all the single malts, rare bourbons, vintage wines, sherries, and port under padlock. As only bottles of ropy spirit, still-burnt rum and dreg wine were kept on display in an old saloon cabinet beside a mercury wall mirror to watch yourself get totally "roostered" in. For there was no simple evening at Davy's Bar, dragged into the dips of dawn and fuck knows were else. For if you weren't skunk-drunk jagged by the time you left Davy's Bar, you probably drank for all the wrong reasons.

And like a sacred vortex, Davy's Bar became "thee place" for all-kinds-of battered, rinky-dink, hardworking men to ponder life, play dominoes, deal cards and throw darts into the wall... Singing and slurring along to Davy's country music blues: lonesome songs—fabling the wild, desperado Legends of the West. Davy's Bar, a place for good ole boys to laugh over the "pains" they outgrew—and cry about the "loves" they once knew. Yesss, this sad bungalow world of Davy 'Deuce' was thee perfect place to drown your sorrows. Davy 'Deuce' the man who got me my first job working at Orion Star Shipping:

Recalling dem rosy days: "Monday's" coming off a weekend on 'amarant'; going to work—hair down to my shoulders—trekking in lumberjacks, wearing tight jeans with a v-neck sweater slipped over a tie-dye tee—as chuggin' a biggie I'd be all hell-yeahed—LUNGS clenching the THC pinging the bubbles of Viotriptamine still blipping in the far fields of my nervous system. Cos back in dem days it was all about da drugs, da drugs, da drrrugs, and how stoned you could get. The mechanical blood alive in me like meat fried in raven oil. As HIT in flashback flight everything in electric blue slowed and glowed. Even the red brick houses glowed an electric blue while shadows of hallucinations old stencilled themselves onto blank walls of huge industrial foundries that loomed like silent headstones. Everything weird and lingering in one long drip-eerie mind-fuck endless echo of recurrence within a shifting forever changing construct of being.

Léguvan and I also discovered the virtues of Magma Coolship's *together* *a beer that tasted like mother's milk "Fresh-Off-The-Tit" *everytime*. And in '91 we had our first taste of 'weed' at a Jezem Jainko Youth Camp deep in Ancoda Forest through which the Naviskat River runs deep; back of Texico Town: a pretty coastal burg with coy rustic cabins and lovely sweet streets.

And regarding that 'weed', 'twas a fortuitous encounter that lead us to the magic of the 'godmarrow'. A wise, elderly forest keeper from the Telamosa Flatlands the bestower of the "timeline changing" 'godmarrow'. The old man himself a smoker of willow bark and white sage; kind-to-us. He, living in a big canvas tent was a teller of rich tales about LIFE ON THE EDGE as well as LIFE ON THE RUN. And each night we'd disappear from camp to visit HIM and just listen and learn and watch as he danced to his battery radio, in the haze of a hissing gas lamp. His feet shuffling across floorboards of a floating platform deck, while with palm placed over his breast and eyes closed, he'd be gone in the sweetest of dreams drifting heart-sore for a wife now, alas, 10-years no more.

And some people SPASM after they've fainted. Others calmly rouse—gradually hearing distant echoing sounds like waking up in a tunnel with the rushing of wind blowing out all the cobwebs: "a rise and shine" as pins and needles tingle; spreading all over your body, a sign that you're coming round as with eyes opening; swimming a bit before clearing, you lay there adjusting, staring and taking it all in; having just had your brain rebooted *to which* a feeling then washes over you and a most calming sensation presides. Yep, a weird refreshment indeed.

And when Léguvan and I ran out of weed and gin, we got our kicks this way: fainting one another. The incident taking place at yet another church camp (Saturday night) summertime. And we caused a bit of a stir. Got all the youth intoxicated on "fainting sessions"—instructing them just how it's done: get down on your haunches, put your head between your knees (chin against chest) and take in deep breaths: hyperventilating fast, fifty times. And then, quickly, jump to your feet, tilting your head your back. And either Léguvan or I would be stood behind 'em to press their throats—cutting the blood supply to the brain. And every time they would faint into our arms (the ultimate faith test) as *safely* we'd lay them down on the grass.

And years earlier at another church camp out in Painted Rock Springs (an area known for its thermal waters warmed by pressure heated rocks deep underground that ran at a steady 49.5 degrees Celsius) to our excitement me and Léguvan found a knothole in the girls bungalow. And sneaking a peek we caught them in the nude and witnessed the ugly-prudence pre-pubescent girls possess—looking as they did like absolute freaks.

And we could've been no more than 12 or 13-years ourselves—giggling in our unquenchable adventure to spy on fresh flesh, as these bubbly creatures; we knew as girls, with ticklish meat still melting; morphing—their teeth too big for their smiles—and bodies, faces still not fully formed darted around squealing like wet piglets - covering up their exposed bits while us boys; now an expanded group of eight, laughed and chanted and carried on - gathered around that sacred peephole (taking turns to spy)—getting an eyeful as the fat ones wobbled like pudding on a cold plate, and the skinny ones darted around like dickless boys.

But with not even the slightest hint of "pubic mound" to sink our rock-hard boners into, these girls sadly appeared as boring as luncheon meat. Not a single whiff of tempting drizzlings. For these weren't the grand firework starters or sexual pulse racing magnetismz our hot squirting dreams were made of. No siree— for with crotches as unattractive as a 14-year-old boy's fluffy top lip these unstimulating creatures were by no means the confident porn mag heroines we spent our lunch breaks ogling over, sat on the bad back steps of Red Valley School—hidden out with the roaring boys who spat and swore and cupped farts into their hands—releasing their little cheezers: ripe gas clouds of reek, into our unsuspecting faces - as turning away too late - we'd bag-up laughing, wheezing like old ugly men.

* * *

And so like this, Léguvan and I shared a friendship deeper than matrimonial night, a life lighter than classical day. For everything we did together was in brotherhood, as ritualistically, each night after celebrating our good friendship; following a truesome night out that often carried on right up until the early bells of morn - drilled on puff and suffering the munchies, we'd kick awake the local gas station attendant to open-up-shop—just so we could grab our favorite microwaved peppersteak pies—devouring them like home-cooked pussy - sauntering back home as thermals from the red rising sun like syrup from a lozenge dropped in boiled water radiated through the undulating tangerine sky.

Yep, Léguvan and I, a great golden duo. We hitchhiked the legendary byways of Māratopia together. We dabbled in mind-altering psychedelic drugs.

7.

SEVENTH SEAL SOCIETY CHURCH

NOW taking any eye-opening substance or "psychedelic compound" should be appreciated and approached as an experiment—a means to cross the chasm, to burn the boat, to glimpse into the abyss, and dissect the plan—busting open the head of creation that one may use the knowledge of the "trip's" core to understand our own hidden nature.

Research on the subject of taking a hallucinogenic substance needed a solid foundation. Hence, the Anzakian writer, Alvis Boman, became our guru.

Boman, a philosophical mystic and a father of modern thought was responsible for the brilliant transcription: "The Color of Drugs" after an experience under the psychedelic drug Salpridin. His account held fundamentals of the visionary experience. For Boman saw psychedelics as a means to experience extraordinary states of consciousness—allowing people who are not mystics, saints or great artists, to have a visionary experience. Amarantium Viotriptamine for Boman was a key to opening new doors of perception: chemical keys, besides other "door openers" such as meditation, solitude, fasting, etc.

"The Color of Drugs" was a meaningful creedence of one man's first hallucinogenic "trip" in captivating detail. Boman's experiences with hallucinogens leading him to see the brain as a "reducing valve"—protecting us against the vast cosmic input of info, which otherwise would flood and overload our everyday consciousness. Hence, the function of the brain is to reduce all available information—locking us into a limited experience of the world. However, Amarantium Viotriptamine frees us from this restriction—opening us to a much larger experience of the world. And so for both Léguvan and I—Boman's enlightened words were like food—provoking and enriching us—making us anxious to try out the prospect of seeing: "Life as a glorious freak out, an original thought perceived perfectly..." (excerpt from: The Color of Drugs by Alvis Boman).

* * *

San agreed to organize us the merchandise. He knew a reliable drug connection who operated around Arroyo Market: a stretch of cobblestone laid in the 1700s as a farmer's market that nowadays is the site for Backwood's most multi-cultural and vibrant flea markets.

Waiting for San—I browsed reads at my favorite second-hand bookstall run by a man with a fat mustachio who smoked pipe and poured coffee; from what seemed like a bottomless flask, into his body all-day-long. And when San finally returned—handing me the stuff, just by his ecstatic behavior: excited for me: blood for blood, bone for dice, trick for fire—I could tell he had scored something genuinely special: *Violaceous Novatross ("blotter amarantium" fresh from Tirzan). But whatever that meant at the time I was totally unaware.

Arriving home—immediately I hid the "blotter amarantium"—keeping it safe in a cool, darkened place.

Getting to sleep that night was near impossible. For restless like a kid the night before the first day of school a belly rush of butterflies kept me wide awake. Giggles shivering through me like trickling streams of pure delight as ducking under the covers I felt high and happy just thinking about what lay in store next day.

* * *

September 1992—Saturday, the day had finally arrived. All the investigations from the literature read on the subject of psychedelics made me pretty confident. All the stories retained from San Cotton's hailed catalog of hallucinogenic experiences made me anxious, as I got ready and dressed for church.

Rocking up at the grounds of the Seventh Seal Society Church, Auburn Hills—Léguvan and I from a distance must have appeared like two villainous marauders; straight out of a Western dime novel, all but ready to pull a raid on some small quiet town.
　*And so with the decision to drop the "amarant" after church, it meant we'd have the whole afternoon to "trip" and fry our brains.

* * *

09:30 am - the Mission Story began. Those from 16-years upward congregating to pay heart, mind and soul testimonies to what some folk deem as **acts of God** that really is just intention and awareness maintained on a plateau of graditude. A constant energetic focus the traction that becomes the driving force. And often when this energy is wielded (a clear signal having been sent) things manifest almost instantaneously which is what religious-heads call "A Move of God", the moment when consciousness or the field of intelligent energy forgets itself and believes it is you; creation at it's utmost. And so with the right teachings on how to tap into this mystic science, stepping into this realization becomes second nature. Cos really what are we but a powerful dream within the mind of the all encompassing energetic field that some refer to as God.

10:00 am - Léguvan and I along with the rest of the youth split from the congregation for the Lesson Study. Adults remaining in the church while we trudged across to the hall next door.

And to our surprise the lesson exploded *insight!* The lesson giver a loose cannon in the church, who lied about being restored in the faith, only to get a message out to the youth. A message that screamed: 'Run for your lives!'—details about how the Sad Book, that bad backstabbers Mad Book was nothing but a fat rip-off. The whole religious thing nothing but a fabrication created off the legacies and heroes from the Golden Land.

And then our lesson giver dropped the big one - a truth bomb that blew all our minds as he broke it to us that even Jezem Jainko himself; the token god of our religion, and god of the new world, was nothing more than an anthropomorphic hailing of the sun - a repackaged deity sold as an upgraded version of a previous god-man stole from the ancient kingdom of Kayset.

And just when we thought our minds couldn't be blown wider, our lesson giver ripped right into us, going: "You better discern what's up, cos what you thought was truth, is all just a pack of lies. Lies that have been in the mix for thousands of years. I mean they've had time, so they've been able to dump this shit so it seems natural or something. I mean they know exactly what it takes to brainwash a culture - all you have to do is bullshit a generation, and after that, their offspring will take to that bullshit like a fish goes to water. The belief will become so ingrained, that the believer will actually think that their tradition was given to them by a god—or some shit like that. But hey, you cannot blame these numb-fucks, all they know what to do, is to "shut up, play dumb and *just* believe".

The lesson giver cooking our brains with his hot licks of wisdom, going: "Be careful, this stuff called religion will mess with your head *for sure* if you buy into it. Biggest gaslighting operation ever, religion. Why they'll even make you question if you scratch your head in the right way. Biggest bunch of fuckers ever, them religious tards - they'll mindfuck you into submission, muddle your intuitions about right and wrong, and make you ashamed of who you want to be, to the point you'll be walking around in a glum trance, parroting their words like an idiot."

But the truth awaits everyone at some point in time, these tired old mind-programming systems nearing their end. And when it all comes tumbling down, a lotta people are gonna lose their shit. Especially the ones still romancing and banging the myth, tch, tch, tch, fucking sad, maan. It's what you could call the single biggest goddamn psyop on the human consciousness, if you ask me. The 'old hands', them sly Draco motherfuckers responsible for creating a symbolic fictional figure, which is nothing more than a representation of every single human being on this planet, and convinced people to bow down, worship kiss it's ass. Real infantile bullshit behaviour. And this illness runs deep, cos now you got billions of bouncy clowns all looking up towards this ficticious saviour godman like he's gonna come down to wipe your bum and change your nappies. They got people looking everywhere for the answer instead of searching within themselves. And if that ain't a major fuck up right there, what is. I mean even to this day, you got some balls deep hardcore believers still waiting on a motherfucker to drop out the sky (riding on a white horse and all) to whisk them off to *that glorious land [Way up high]*. Jezem Jainko the current title holder - having had the longest running orgasm in history - for HE still coming; haaard! Ha, ha, damn (shaking his head) now if that ain't some silly ass buffoonery right there, I don't know what is. Grown ass sheeple still believing in the lie they were told as a child. Fuck me! Mankind is done for if we continue to be this dumb, waiting on some deliverer to pluck you from your sad, miserable, fucked up situation. Shieet! Doesn't anyone get it though, the fact that NO FUCKING SAVIOUR IS COMING TO REDEEM YO ASS, MUTHAFUKKA!! You are here all on your own, for it is you, and you alone, who has to **FIND A WAY OUTTA HERE!** So soldier the fuck up, cuzzy... cos ain't no sky daddy saviour Jeze Bob gonna be shooting down no chimney pipe for the soul purpose of pinning yo useless ass with angel wings, dammit! So just shut down that burdensome head buzz of guilt and inferiority and step up to the fucking plate, bitch!"

And after that we all looked at one another, shell-shocked; the lesson giver continuing: "And so now you know the truth."

And after that everyone was like "So what the fuck do we do now?" And the lesson giver told us: "There still are rulesets to observe here in this murky realm, so I'd advise you not to get too reckless with your life; know what I mean. Just use your intuition as the ultimate guide to reading the Universe. You'll know it when you've hit the sweet spot, it's when 'that spark' of true connection between heart and mind, that totally blissed out state, unfolds, that essence of being, maan, walking the ancient path like a true Jedi. Cos look here, at the end of the day, it's all just about alignment with self. And alignment with is alignment with the intelligent energy we all are apart of, which boils down to self-acceptance and the acceptance of others. And so, if you can keep all that in mind, you ain't got nothing to worry about, for the Universe will always have your back as long as you're carrying yourself in truth and are not harming others, then you are gold. And beyond that, well, what else can I say other than have no regrets about the process—just learn to admire it and how precious it all is. And also remember to meditate every day, it's the key to keeping a clear head; you know, get down deep in there to seperate yourself from what is not yourself: the ego, allowing all them attachments to fall by the wayside. And other than that, just be - observe, absorb, flow and find your own truth, no Gods or god-men or self appointed men of prophecy needed. It's just you and your connection with self, now get the fuck outta here!"

And after that lesson on awareness we spilled out into the church grounds and breathed in the brave new intoxicating day—soaking the sun into our skins - the celebration of Spring all around - butterflies flapping like petals of light, as a hungry chick wet out the egg fell to the ground, eaten by ants, while radiant flowers, open like oysters, gargled drops of radiant dew as lustrous as moonstone blue. And off concrete walls, the sunlight it beams over your face as all you can do, eyes closed with a smile, is drown in its warm flooding embrace—feeling that liquid love all mixed up inside your body and soul melt. And at the foot of the Dellameer Mountain Range, rocking in the red ragged heat, the cool Spring tide swollen like a fiery gonad *pumps* as salt crystals star-burst on sturdy flats like sparkling sperm, while waves break and beach and swash and fizzle into fertile shores.

* * *

And so digging the sun, Léguvan and I: two rebel-stone boys with unpracticed cool and bad-undertones—hung chatting with the lovely barelegged fresh Jezem Jainko cult girls: all a-blush and giggling, hooked on our every word - their feet a-fidgeting—wanting to run away and burn-out their inner wickednesses on us. Fingers a-fumbling frocks—touching their most delicate intimacies - unaware of how sexy they were—looking up at us with big daisy lashes and eyes dreamy pleading for blissful sex beneath rich blue skies, left breathless, lying upon a golden field of some ravished land glazed in sweat and tears of joy - dresses hiked up—exposing the glittery blood sparkling within the virgin wound.

And just then, a lanky shadow loomed over my shoulder giving me the shudders as jolt of the heebie-jeebs crawled all over my flesh like a cluster of tarantulas. It was the head elder - there to remind us we both were on deacon duty. A slight detail that in our buzzed-out anticipation of tripping balls we somehow overlooked.

* * *

Now deacon duty on Holy Communion day involves putting out chairs in a big circle. And then in front of each chair a foot basin is placed. Two buckets are filled with water. One bucket placed in the foot washing area for women. The other in an area for men. Water from the buckets are jugged into the foot basins (halfway). Then members of the congregation pair up. One sits with feet in basin, the other kneels. Both bow heads. The person kneeling utters a pray, washes the seated person's feet—and vice versa.

After foot washing the Main Ceremony starts. Deacons offer the congregation unleavened bread: a symbol for the flesh of their mythic god, and unfermented wine as its blood.

We sat through Divine Service, held just before everyone divided for foot washing, and figured since Divine Service started at 11:00 am—lasting 45 minutes, that we'd take the "amarant" just after—which would give us approximately 35 min before the stuff kicked in—allowing us to attend foot washing and perform our deacon duties for the Main Ceremony without any slip-ups.

* * *

'See you on the other side.' were the indelible words as Léguvan Tiggs and I in the gents cubicle of the Auburn Hills Seventh Seal Society Church, dropped "amarant".

We kept the blotting paper beneath our tongues until the texture turned pulpous, like chewed-up tissue paper. Then we swallowed. Our tongues numb as if having licked a 9Volt battery.

20 min later we joined the men. And by this time I already began to feel something queer lurking within. The drug was coming up fast, binding, I guess, with the serotonin receptors in my brain, as in a sudden rush of blood to the head, I became aware of a detachment I had never felt before. My whole mood elevated as if everything I was seeing was for the first time. My new world had just begun.

* * *

Now communion foot washing is nothing like doing the dishes or soaking your sweaty ballsack or scrubbing out your girl's cherry-blood or boyfriend's shit-oil from last night's sheets (terrified ye momma's gonna find out). No, it's meant to be meaningful. A bonding-act between your fellow church brethren. And as fate would have it, I got paired up with the head elder: a bald, God-fearing, hymn-whistling religious diehard prick—called Uncle Willie - who smelt of mothballs, shoe shine and death-breath. And before washing Uncle Willie's feet, I knelt down and said a prayer for him, his sad anemic wife, and their weezing angelic son with one lung; wondering what in the fucks name was I doing there.

And for sure, by now, the "amarant" was graduating through me like an exceptionally fine rhapsody. An ominous tear-up of old forms stabbing at my perception, as beneath a formidable black sky; prepped out and charged up, all Ready, Set, Go!—rocking & heaving, roaring & seething—I got catapulted UNBOUND riding the flashes of portal thunders deep within the mystery of worlds unexplored—as all of a sudden, entering upon an open field *BA-BOOM!* lit-up alive by a wild cascading energy, I continued to soar. The heartbeat of my skull pulsating pressure as a nine-inch cut spike *POW!* got driven through my cortex: a sledgehammer-shot of regeneration that delivered home my new self straight onto the altar of death and reawakening. And so like this, with my supersoul received, as a newborn-stone-rebel; the hope of many - set against the grain of the old world and bent to the stars, I secretly convulsed as wildcats and sidewinders moaned voodoo magic through me.

After the first wave of the drug had settled down, somewhat doe-eyed, I looked upon the people in that cramped little room and was met with a sickening feeling that hit me *WHACK!* like a punch straight to the sternum; altering my rhythm-flow. At once, in that realisation, I understood that HERE: within this nerve center of *religio*—with all its traditionalism: the rituals, the observed days; the strong "wannabeism", that it was nothing more than a cult for people who attracted bad vibes. And so right there, I understood. I saw it. The root of the deception. The way they projected their own spiritual deformity onto those deemed unsaved, in order to justify their self-limiting beliefs. It was nothing more than a roundabout attempt at proving through their scripted role-play, that they were the chosen ones, and everyone else that did not accept their message was doomed. It was all a big bag of bullshit.

That's when I realized my life's mission. In that moment I knew I would have to be the one responsible for driving the stake through the heart of *religio*. It was that simple, it was that hard. Freddy Snakes the zombie killer, Freddy Snakes the vampire slayer: a free man evolved and cut off from the herd. But in checking myself for just a second, I pondered: *"Isn't this though how all religio's are formed, by visions of election and grandeur."* And so I held back on myself, but through the darkness within, through the uncertainly, an answer like a star cut through the doubt as now with this new truth sat comfortably beneath my skin - something had settled and connected, and right then I knew I was a different person. But what would I do with this new insight? How would I wield this realisation. For it was as though something strange, yet familiar, almost of a higher vibrational presence, had began to vibrate within me at a cellular level, that burned through my old self a light, penetrating now into the consciousness of each person as I saw each one of their past lives, their dreams, their darkest secrets. I was unprepared for such bold insight. Something strange was taking over for sure. An unceasing frequency all too much that weighed heavily upon my body and mind; downloads of pure intel that literally pressed me down. For by taking this drug, turning this portal key, I had allowed something access to my very being. It was the case of too much, too soon—for having not built a solid foundation for such new insight—I literally did not account for being savagely mauled alive like some cognisant ragdoll, while same time being pumped full with a spontaneity of bright, euphoric data that literally blew my mind. It was a fresh declaration, that as I stood there and stared, literally began unprogramming and reconfiguring me. I was being made into a whole new vessel, a modern weapon for the war against the old order: an awakened convert deep undercover for an imminent covert strike.

Indeed, I had now seen the hidden nasty heart of this ragged religious order—of which, so many times, I had been unconsciously apart of. The men of this "poison-doctrine cult" now performing their ritualistic foot washing, muttering emptiness, as they spoke over one another with hands rested reassuringly upon shoulders and backs, like some weird close-knit Turkish bath sorority of brokeback pains, seedy deals and shit-pushing in the dark. The lot of 'em thick as a knot, with just one heartbeat between, as with souls shallow as graves they appeared to me now like members of some cut-throat cult. The very breath I drew stifled by the realisation that every man there was aid to the circle—the circle of secrecy. And then it dawned. Perhaps the Seventh Seal Society Church was not the so-called "Lighthouse at the End of Time" that they made themselves out to be. But rather a covert crusade for wicked dealings. But this would mean that I too was in on the act, like some broken abductee of this strange wintery clan, as now deep-seated in their presence like a fly on the wall, within my revelation of self, I awoke to the floundering fact, that up until this moment, the church had had me suckered and tagged all along. And that all I ever was, was just some bogus meatsuit (with the lights on, but no one at home). The dice, I guess, long ago rolled as down payment for my soul. Them tricky numbers, sealing unconsciousness within. For not one-of-us: the chosen remnant of the Seventh Seal Society Church, seemed like actual people. For it appeared as if my extended family were nothing more than vessels for *spirits of the damned* who had returned to finish the work. Fuck! This Amarantium Viotriptamine was hitting me hard. But not only that. The "something within" that was steering my ascension, was desecrating all my sacred cows—removing the scales from my eyes to reveal the sheer horror I was living.

It was Uncle Willie's turn now to do the honors—kneeling as he did, all ready to wash my feet. But far removed from the situation, I no longer saw him as The Man or Pillar of the Community. There was an off-key magnetism about him. A dark scowl hiding a key secret that hummed beneath his grotesque pride. For there in a clear vision—I caught a glimpse of his little black heart. I peered into his bad dream and saw his deepest secret: the soundproof garage: wall-to-wall with old abused tools - hung on pegboard. Tools that were like his "little buddies". Implements of torture spattered with stipples of blood and sodden with sinew. Stars in a sick performance, such as the oily bench vise that Uncle Willie nicknamed: Clive: used for gripping limbs as he cut them into portions. And Errol: the rusty hacksaw, with a voice of his own—rasping on the ear every time he cut clean through bone. And next to that, Edna: the greasy Vaseline jar, with teeth and gum tissue preserved in brown blood and turpentine. And lastly, the star of the show: Bobby: the grubby ball pein hammer, who did his job well when Uncle Willie smashed him down into the eye socket of the prostitute - now rolled up in a rug and stuffed into the boot of his "Beloved" '66 Valiant Barracuda.

Yep, I saw it all—Uncle Willie's dark secret - and it burned. A burning so bright I could not tear my mind's eye from his hidden gem that glowed like a cinder in the dark. My heart racing sickness as I saw Uncle Willie swing his "Beloved" into the church grounds—smiling to himself behind tinted windows—knowing all's forgiven, as he chauffeured his sick and secret burden, while the kiddies; excited to see him, came running up to the car—leaving sticky little prints all over the darkened windows of his "Beloved" as they tried to peer inside and catch a glimpse of the figure in the dark—just as I have peered into the darkness of Uncle Willie's sick soul. And all that the kiddies want is a chance to be that boy or girl lifted up in Uncle Willie's strong arms and carried into the church like a Lamb of God. And Uncle Willie doesn't mind the attention. In fact, he relishes it. Because nobody knows his "power secret", therefore he's all right. For he's The Man and a big Uncle to everyone, as everyone loves Uncle Willie—everyone except me. And then, continuing to peer into the void, I saw after church service, Uncle Willie manoeuvre his big "Beloved" homeward, followed by the kiddies—all of them hailing screams down the road after him—not wanting him to go. But they don't understand - for they don't see Uncle Willie smirking to himself in his rear view mirror—knowing his secret burden is safe.

And then, peering even deeper into Uncle Willie's tinted horror like the kid who gazes longingly at the last sad puppy in the pet store window. The puppy no one wants because he is a sick pup (swallowed up by disease), I realized, all that time, I had been peering into the eternal darkness of my own sick soul.

POOF! suddenly I looked down and there was Uncle Willie washing my feet. What a servile little cock-scrubber, I thought, wait, what?! Did I really think that, I thought ... was this me? A low vibration reeling through my head, as biting my lip, I almost burst into tears of manic laughter—the "amarant" doing a switch-up on me—as right then - totally open to the beauty of the moment - I didn't know whether to spit or jerk-off over Uncle Willie's baldpate in payment for his humble servitude. Woah, there? I tried to slow things down, to perhaps listen to my thoughts, but could barely realize anything. And then in an instant *KA-BOOM!* another wave of intensity hit me. The Amarantium Viotriptamine screaming through me as a riot-treasure of alternate realities, popping off like an arcade of neons, spooled over the arc light shimmering within my brain, as that blissful drug now firing on all cannons pushed me to find the spaces of my psyche not yet colored in. For like Captain of the Dead; my closet a full crew of skeletons doomed to voyage the seven galaxies forever, I played a game of chance; my mind smashed to atoms, as crashing down my spine orgasmic lukewarm waterfalls wailed sirens that filled me up like a golden chalice brimming sweet angelic tears *from the sighs* glad sorrow. And then in an instant *SHOEM!* everything appeared normal.

40 odd minutes into the "trip" and already my world was turning wonderfully topsy-turvy. The drug: in one emotion: "fucking ludicrous", as looking to the other end of the room—I saw Léguvan freaking out. Just another idiot in the idiot brigade—a man with a bus ticket, but no destination in mind. And just then, in that moment, our eyes locked and we both clicked and realized we had to maintain cool heads. For we still had to get through communion service—and eight hours

or so of solid balls-out tripping. It was gonna to be a colorful, fairground kinda day.

After communion foot washing all the men stood in a big linked circle like a rugby scrum, and as a blessing, the pastor said a prayer, while Léguvan and rolled our eyes and gnashed our teeth.

8.

SARATOKA PLAINS

THE Field of Storms rolled and romped her busty waves that *Ker-ashed!* on the adrenaline shoreline—forming seductive mermaids in pretty iridescent fish scale tights, true goddesses of sexual love; born from a sea of foam—anchor-roped into sparkling embraces with thunderous ghost sailors: tattooed turquoise with veins stuck-out undulant over bulging biceps, as making maritime love they boomed and shot up in salted spray.

* * *

Up Mesacola Trail with a one-track-mind, I made my way back home to the house on the hill in Sweet Place village—"The Seeds of Surprise" wrapped in foil paper and concealed in a box of matches, stashed in the inner pocket of my Granddaddy's battered old desert coat.

It was a wet winter's night, shivery like goose flesh on a high-heeled whore; in a plastic raincoat, with nothing more than the will to live and a cigarette for company, as the wind, blowing howls through trees that hid in the dark, lashed raindrops into my face the size of giant marbles that flew down and shattered to the ground like stained glass soap bubbles.
    And nearing my territory I caught the nagging voice of fate on every damp gust welcome me into the realm of Saratoka Plains: home of Mount El Morro and my adventure playground since age-5.
    In my growing up years Saratoka Plains was a place bursting with life: untouched and wild—OVERGROWN with dense clusters of Mesquite and Blackbrush, including many species of grass, plants and weed. And every day I'd disappear for hours

on end to explore and bird-spot and build bonfires the size of archways—jumping through giant flames in celebration of LIFE that is the "Spark" within. And when the sky became bruised, and the swifts and swallows were out swooping and diving, and the massive yellow moon hung low in the big indigo sky... My mother would stand at the crest of the slope that led down into the wilderness of Saratoka Plains, and call: 'Freddy, supper's ready!' But I'd never go indoors and would play until supper got cold and had to be reheated in the oven.

* * *

Saratoka Plains attracted many bird species and became a local sanctuary. Every bird indigenous to the Western region visited Saratoka Plains—from the orange-faced Weaver, with its *Azwit, azwit* calls. To the Masked Weaver, wearing its tiny little Lone Ranger mask. To Lapwings and Killdeer that would go berserkers if you happened to wander near their clutch of eggs with rasping metallic nags. And there'd also be the red-cheeked Pheasant, who'd appear on our front lawn - ten to fifteen of them (summertime) under the sprinkler—bathing and cooling off. And sometimes joining them, a small convoy of Spotted Wood-Quail—with their tiny chicks falling in line. And with its big Bambi-eyes—batting sweet lashes, the darling Mourning Dove. While the dear Sparrow with his little jerky chirps would chirrup—as in amongst twigs and leaves, hopping briskly—looking for flies, bugs, and lizards - the noble Robin would sound: *Cherooo-weeeet*. And stilted between rasping reeds with its puffed-out cobra-like head—the Blue Impereon, living insignia of Māratopia, would rattle with a high-pitched punctuated *Kraaaarrrk!* While often with its distinctive calls, the dear Mockingbird would call like a grand old father of Māratopia.

And many more birds lived in Saratoka Plains, such as the Canary, Bulbul, Francolin, Reed Warbler, Black Kite, Sugarbird, Meadowlark, Red-winged Starling, and the White-Eye with its reedy little notes that *Pew-pew, Pew-pewed*, as buzzing *Dzzzttt-*

dzzzt-dzzzt the Shrike, cousin of the butcher bird, would swoop down chasing all the other birds. And then my favorite feathered friend, who's really an angel, the Wagtail—always bobbing around the garden—checking things out like a little proud marcher. And let's not forget that hooded virtuous fool: the Hoopoe, who'd make its special appearance every once in a while. And what about the Speckled Pigeon, and the Nightjar, the Swallow, and Swift—yesss—every one of these wonderful little friends—ALL were contained within the realm of Saratoka Plains.

And when the big rains came and the water table rose, a huge expanse or wetland of the bluest blue stood and remained and got named Bucks Dam. And for seven great years '89 to '96—it was haven to hundreds of nesting water birds. Birds such as the Sacred Ibis and Coot, the Mallard, and White Faced Duck, the Branta Goose, Black-Necked Grebe, the Teal, Common Gull, the Shoveler, the Yellow Billed Duck, the Reed Cormorant, the Kingfisher - you name it - they all loved Bucks Dam.

Saratoka Plains also had a good collection of small creatures like the Skink Lizard, Sand Frog, Sand Toad, and Tortoise. There were also insects such as the Dragonfly, the Pond Skater, the Water Scavenger Beetle, Horse Fly, Lady Bug, the May Beetle, Darkling Beetle, Stink Bug, Pleasant Hornet, Blister Beetle, Fruit Beetle, the Tarantula, Locust, Grasshopper, Cricket, Praying Mantis, plus many more... Including rodents like the Striped Field Mouse, the Stoat, the Golden Mole, and the Jackrabbit. And my personal favorite—the largest mammal that lived in Saratoka Plains—the White-tailed Deer.

The Saratoka Plains had its fair share of serpents too. Snakes like the Sand Boa. The Prairie Rattlesnake. The Northern Copperhead. The Brown Cruset, and my all-time favorite, the Western Redjewel—king snake of the Saratoka Plains.

And back then it was common to find a Redjewel in your property. Stories fanning about the neighborhood of so-and-so who saw a Redjewel in their backyard, or that aunty who caught one in her kitchen; drinking from the cat's water bowl. Everyone at some point in the early days of Sweet Place having had run-ins with the Western Redjewel. The villagers were terrified and suffered nightmares of being bitten. And many times in my sleep I died in poisoned dreams—especially after it spread that someone found a Western Redjewel curled up in their shoe, beneath their bed.

And throughout my life on Saratoka Plains, on more than one occasion, I stood toe-to-toe with the Western Redjewel. And the person who knows this well and true is my good Uncle Lonnie Mankali: my mom's curly, blonde, half-brother. Uncle Lonnie Mankali the cleverest person I've ever met. And being somewhat of an older brother to me (by 5-years) Uncle Lonnie led me by the hand (into everything we got up to) in them yearling-days between infancy and puberty. And from the time we lived out in the suburb of Nakamosa... we met many weird and wonderful incarnations. Uncle Lonnie at the time homed in a block of flats in Ravine Heights. His next door neighbor a real menace, nicknamed Periwinkle: a flamed-haired little shit, who wore suspenders and thick specs, who'd throw his cat Cheeto over the balcony from the 10th floor (every day)—amazed at how it could land on its feet (each time) and survive. Until one day the poor animal just gave up on luck - landing with a *SPLAT!* And as cats don't die easy - the poor thing went into a 20 minute epileptic fit - its eyeballs all popped out and body rattling with a wheezing sigh. Hence the reason we avoided Periwinkle. But another boy, Chase, he was a cool vibrating presence. He and Uncle Lonnie, naughty—but clever-naughty (ingenious in fact) catching harmless snakes and painting them with Airfix enamels—setting them loose in the courtyard, hidden in wait, giggling, as they heard the 'shriekings' of girls who did wee-wees in their panties, and the 'wailings' of old aunties who swooned limp-wristed—shrinking at the sight of them colorful voodoo-like serpents; darting tongues smooth as erotic fire.

And not far from Uncle Lonnie I lived with my mom and dad in a blue and white bungalow that had a water pump out back and a hedge out front: covered in meleons: a name my dad and I gave chameleons. And there'd be grandpa-meleons, and grandma-meleons, and baby-meleons... And you needn't look hard in them days—always several in a tree or on a bush. And the same went for geckos and lizards—nature was in abundance in those days. Māratopia's suburbs back then rich and vibrant with such wildlife.

Now the bungalow my folks rented was owned by a mad, sun-struck Nambian, who lived two doors down, who my daddy nicknamed 'El Rilla the Mower'—cos all 'Mower' did all day was mow his blessed lawn and break into hot vinegary sweats—standing-Grecian—leaned up against his front wall like proud marble... Admiring his day's labor—sipping ice-cold Marshall's soda pop in the sticky sun with big ugly freckles on his heavy muscular back - greeting the neighbors, along with the postman, and milkman, as the perfect little dimension of Nakamosa revolved and sailed around the cascading day.

But soon we had to turn our backs on the suburb of Nakamosa. Both Uncle Lonnie's parents and mine deciding to buy property elsewhere out on Saratoka Plains in an area called Sweet Place - which became the frontier of our new lives.

* * *

And a typical day in Sweet Place spent with Uncle Lonnie Mankali's parents: Ma Cookie: my grandmother and her second husband: my step-granddaddy: Uncle Reggie Mankali—would regimentally begin with Uncle Reggie waving goodbye to us—always with a lit (crush pack) Tribetex Red coolly tucked in the corner of his mouth; his one eye slit, to prevent it watering, as he rumbled off in his '69 AMC Rambler—heading to his job as "typesetter" at the Māratopia Times in the heart of Backwood on Smoke Street, one of the oldest streets in Māratopia, known for its vibrant printing and publishing offices.

Yesss. Good ole Uncle Reggie, who lost his Satnakian-blooded dad in the War of Broken Wills, 1942—keeping in his shirt pocket the same bullet-holed, bloodstained black-and-white of him on his mother's arm that his daddy carried over his heart, the day he got gunned down by the enemy.

Yep, poor hard luck Uncle Reg, who after only a year of retirement got rocked 1. by a bad investment and 2. a hidden past that got dug up. The first blow came when a conman with a perm made off with Uncle Reg's entire nest egg. And so drilled sick with worry and stress it broke Uncle Reg down, as storming and thundering in maddening flashes and fits of fury—Uncle Reg vowed to find the nasty peckerwood responsible for swindling him out of his investment; intent on killing the fool. This being the season when Uncle Reg raced across the countryside; a loaded gun in his cubby-hole, ready to deal out bare justice. He really wanted that guy so badly he literally saw him everywhere. But unfortunately Uncle Reg had to call off his little manhunt, after chasing down some random dude with a perm; nearly killing the poor bastard. This close call leading Uncle Reg to assess just how far over the edge he had really gone. Uncle Reg swerving off to the side of the road, hunched over the steering wheel in tears. His search for justice at a close.

And then the final blow. A box arrived at Uncle Reg's doorstep, posted from Pondesa, town of Uncle Reg's birth. This already an ominous sign. Uncle Reg having not had contact with anyone (no family or friends) from that heavy day he left Pondesa Town in '69, to shack up and brood over Ma and her big belly.

And for a good part of the day Uncle Reg just sat at the kitchen table; a cup of coffee evaporating beside a sideplate of Lemon Creams, staring at the unopened parcel in the middle of the table, contemplating its potential contents, as if what lay within held an energy that could create a fracture in his current perception, that could effectively sending him off on a trajectory that would have him spiralling down an alternate timeline of oblivion.

And so, unable to wait anymore, taking a deep breath, Uncle Reg lifted the lid off that time-bomb - the result of which sent a shockwave through the quantum realm. The contents consisting of 1. a small wooden box that held an old 2-shot Derringer (pocket pistol) 2. the War of Broken Wills service medal that belonged to his daddy and 3. love letters.

The letters covered the period from when Uncle Reggie's mom and dad first met, up until when correspondence between the two lovers ceased. The letters revealed hidden family secrets. Uncle Reggie's dad having come from a wealthy family. But when his family found he was dating a woman from the poor side of town, the *whole* family disowned him. And then when Uncle Reggie's dad died fighting in Dohan, his poor mom, without support, fell into the arms of another man, who ended up becoming Uncle Reg's step-father: a violent drunk who beat his wife and step-son. Uncle Reggie, one day, beaten-up so badly by his step-father, that severe nerve damage to Uncle Reggie's face left him cockeyed.

And so like a landslide of shit and thunder it all came tumbling down. And out of the flames of his own life—a new Uncle Reg was born: the man we eventually all got to know as Uncle Jove—for Uncle Reggie was no more. It was Uncle Jove who had won the battle of wits.

And so, as our family's very own "pioneer of awakening"— in the prime of his breakthrough; jabbering and cookin' up some next complex divine thing—Uncle Jove would spazz out, often bobbing his head, arm jerking, to which jumping up, he'd go: 'Are you fuckin' twisted or something, brachie?!' Or 'Yo! Ass maimer! You suck!' But sometimes, sat peaceful on the doorstep, watching folks go by—he'd snigger into his armpit, and pulling and jerking, would shout: 'Oh, you lucky bastard, look at you!' And yes—often, Uncle Jove, deeply immersed in the void, would rattle off; rough-toned—going on about *how* every dimension is a construct of the perfect thought. And how everything is assisting this perfect intelligent intention, for the purpose that it may realize itself, to the point that one day, when it finally does reach a full realization of self—or when it finally does get to see its own face, that it will simply cease to exist, a complete reset. Everything resorting back to nothingness - back to pure potential.

And I recall the time Uncle Jove—driving in peak traffic— with my mom as shotgun. And paying no heed to the other vehicles—he veered across lanes—pulling up on the roadside;

almost causing a pile-up, just to check some leather purses and handbags a vendor was selling. And after choosing a purse for Ma, Uncle Jove paid the vendor with a sweet and just walked off like nothing had happened; purse tucked under arm—while the guy, drop-jawed, looked on in blank disbelief. My mother having to pay for Uncle Jove's faux pas.

Another time of legendary self-searchings—concerning the case of Uncle Jove: was when Ma witnessed him launch into thrashing fits and lucid nightmares—babbling like a cooked-up loon (lost to the moon), vortex'd in their sheets—raving at the top of his glorious skull like a beast prophet—going on about some awful black divination in his bulging skull. For it was within this break through season that Uncle Jove became the "Bearer of Light". He had received his awakening - unplugged fully from this reality to become a thunderbolt in a storm cloud. Uncle Jove, the hammer of justice that the 9th dimension had been searching for, in execution of the overthrowal those he deemed: "the crafty ones—the ones kindling the flame of the Old Order, and who hold the keys to the Portal of Change. Them "old hands" manipulating the frequency of the planet; along with the timelines of this murky (3D) realm. And so, such downloads Uncle Jove inscribed on crumpled bits of paper - all safeguarded and stuffed into the self-same pillowcase he'd mutter and drool on each night, as visions of The Premonitions of Dawn and The Looming Age of the Skull gripped him deeply. For he could be found often labouring for hours with pen and paper over such cryptograms of individuation: lifted in gripping states of wholeness—dripping sweat by penlight clenched between teeth, buzzing in a haze of gasoline fumes and cut grass, stowed in the mower shed, as he underwent the agonies of awakening and insightful perception.

And eventually; ritualistically, Uncle Jove began spending all his time shacked up in that "Godforsaken mower shed"- right up until the breakings of dawn—shivering in a hypnotic state, being possessed by ecstatic visions in the diluted darkness—body streaming perspiration, eyeballs bulged, skin glistening, as he wrote with intense energy and frantic reason—likening a soul-raped man: sick, and set on fire—pulling pen across paper like a plough across fertile fields, sowing seeds—watering the earth with life-giving sweat, coughing and sucking rags doused in accelerant—as he scrawled with passion purpose like a man knowing the exact stamp of his demise.

And it was here, in gloom of the mower shed, at the peak of his transcendence; face glowing enlightenment, when Uncle Jove, inscribing the penultimate paragraph of his breakthrough; the Buddha flame already dancing above his head now, did receive the climax of his life's work deep in a trance of what was an "earth-shaking" revelation of self: the universe having finally opened her glory to him.

And as a result of this carry-on, Ma thought a demon had crawled up inside of Uncle Jove. And in a panic she dialled the church leader who deployed his deacons - boys stomping over in suits and ties; all smug with bibles under their arms—holding out tracts—encouraging Uncle Jove to get re-reborn - as "It wasn't too late for his devil hide to be saved." And at the time, Uncle Jove, dressed in nothing but a gown and flip flops; his balls swinging like a heavy sack of nuts, was busy barbecuing some homemade bean burgers, flipping 'em over with an egg turner, when these deacons, wet out the womb, came up barking scripture in the hope of herding Uncle Jove's lost soul back to God—not expecting their words to be like a match to the fuel of Uncle Jove's already rampant derision. As foaming at the mouth he rebuked them—raging and blasting them out with sheer volume, going: 'I don't wanna be hearing no bullshit now about no Jeze Bob Jainko, you hear me!'

Them boys cautious, going: 'Sir, can't we at least say a prayer for you.'

Uncle Jove almost ready to explode at their sass, going: 'Looks like you knuckleheads are adamant to fuck up my day, aren't ye? Probably got orders from the top, huh? Signed and sealed by Brekem Young himself, I bet. Damn! That creepy ass Drakazoid-motherfucker has had a hard-on for me ever since I dropped the soap in the showers at Camp Meeting. So it don't suprise me none, when now, in my divine moment of reflection, that here he is, sending you two dickheads over, bent on railroading me down into his little washed-out circle of worship.' Uncle Jove now looking at both them boys from the side with a wry smile, going: 'So how well you know this pastor of yours?'

Them boys blushing, replying: 'All we know is that he is a real stand up man, sir.'

Uncle Jove giving them a stern looking: 'Tch, yeah, I bet. Maan, you boys are so green, I can literally smell the shit in your pants. Y'all need to be spitting out that blue pill that's got your brain all sheepefied, and take a sip of "wake-the-fuck-up!!", cos there be *bare tings* you need knowing about your creepy leader. Shit that'll make you tremble.'

Them deacons looking at one another now ablush and confounded, not knowing what to think, as Uncle Jove continued:

'Yeah, for real. That pork chop sucking leader of yours, Brekem Young, he down with all kindsa funky ass repugnance. That's why he and the Mrs can't conceive, if you know what I mean.'

The one deacon going: "Sir, what are you saying?"

"What I'm saying is, Brekem Young ain't taking care of his woman like he should be, you feel me?"

And the deacon now possibly inspired by Uncle Jove's zest to peel back the layers on life, and the fact that his own brain had allowed him to figure it out, excitedly blurted out: 'You mean to say that he ain't pounding the pussy?'

'Aha! Now you getting it... he-is-not-pounding-the-pussy.' stressed Uncle Jove, semi-celebrating the lads moment of recognition with a: look-at-you-go look, as Uncle Jove continuing, went: 'And "Why?" you might ask. Well I'll tell you Why. It's because he always out there in dem woods, spending all his time with strange men, getting up to all kinds of fucked-up, nasty shit.' Uncle Jove drawing them boys in with his juicy secret, going: 'Yeah, you better believe dat, straight up facts.' As looking up from them mouthwatering patties, slappin' 'em on buns, Uncle Jove offered them deacons to partake, to which they strongly refused. And so taking a huge bite from his blessed bean burger, Uncle Jove let out a proud-chested gaffawing roar of laughter (crumbs falling caught in his chest hair) as then, searching the eyes of them deacons sent to restore him, Uncle Jove went: 'Mmm-hmm! This be one fine meat free patty, boys, sure you don't want some.'

One of them boys going: 'We come here on a mission to do God's bidding. Not to be tasting your filthy pagan bean burgers, sir.'

Uncle Jove going: 'Yeah? Well you must be as dumb as shit to turn down a handsome offer such as this.' Uncle Jove looking at his bean burger lovingly, going: 'But hold up a second. Did I just hear you summthin' about being on a motherfucking mission from Gaaad?

The deacons replying: 'Why yes, sir. Life is all about doing God's bidding.'

'Have you lost your goddamn mind? Gaaad, huh? Ha ha. You mean the same Gaaad that recruits peeps to be speaking and writing books for it. Yeah, ooofh, sounds like life of the party. The one and only Gaaad almighty, the all powerful overseer that no one ever gets to see. Well, not unless you're checking yo zits in the mirror, right?' Them deacons confounded once more, as Uncle Jove, looking on 'em like they had lifetimes more to learn, went: 'Shieet, I forgot. That info is above your pay grade, ain't it. They don't teach the mystic truths of the universe to no newbie wet ear, do they now. No, they just unleash the text on you, leaving you in your own limited understanding to extract a meaning of some sort, which most the time would be a literalist interpretation, when instead, what they should be doing, is taking time to actually teach you the real mystic, multi-layered hidden meanings, along with where them stories got copied from. But no, they've done so much covering up as to what the truth really that everything is upside down. Just like what they did 2000 years ago when they brand named and personified the intelligent energy of the universe under the household trademark name of Jezem Jainko: latest God-man on the block—or "Gaaad" to the spiritually deformed. Ha! Jokes, huh? Nothing but pompous bullshit. After all, there just ain't no grounding once adopting the imposter's mentality, is there. Why them slave drivers: those Drakazoids, they took what was sacred, twisted it around and fucking turned it into a goddamn cartoon. Sneaky motherfuckers. They always manage to find a way them useless Drakazoids. Taking something honest, pure and truthful, and then defiling it. But that's just how they roll. They're the filth of the world, and unfortunately only a handful can see it - cos most have been programmed since childhood to accept the defiled as being the original or "the truth" - when clearly it is not. Nowadays people are so removed from their own universal truth, hence the reason why they're unable to naturally create or manifest the life they want. I mean; it is your goddamn birthright to be able to do that, but you will never be free to create the life that you want as long as you're still locked into their slave system. They halted everything and disrupted the order of things by poisoning the wells of knowledge - diluting the essential tools left to us by the ancients: the yogis and shamen; the great mystics of the Golden Age—selling nothing but falsehoods and delusion to the clown-sheep out there, who lapping it up as truth, not knowing how deeply entrenched into the slave system they really are, just continue to believe the bullshit and live a lie. Psh! I mean, can't you see it, can't you seen the mindfuck, how they've pulled the wool over your glazed over eyes.'

And them deacons did not know what to say, looking like their minds just got fucked.

'Ooo, yeah, that's it - looks like I may have just hit the spot, so I'll just let that little truth bomb simmer for a while.' chuckled Uncle Jove, biting into another wholesome bean burger, going:

'Now I get that you boys are wanting to stay in your pastor's good books and all, rolling up here with a weird ass agenda that by the looks of it is falling apart at the seams. Cos from the get-go, I bet y'all thought you had it in the bag, didn't ye, rolling up here all suited and booted with bibles under your arms and shit - looking to dish out a slice of brimstone. But all I can say is, shame on you, cos y'all turned up at the wrong motherfucking address. And so now it is on. I'm gonna bust your heads so wide open that you gonna need space in your skull for extra brains. Cos me, I ain't fuckin' around today. So before it gets real nasty, and to save me from humiliating your punk asses, I'll give you the benefit of the doubt, either you stay here and learn or you take that lame ass solar deity Jezem Jainko, along with your weak-ass religion, and get the fuck off my property!'

But them stubborn fools not hearing Uncle Jove, replied:

'Now wait a minute, sir, you need to stop blaspheming and repent!'

But Uncle Jove was having none of it, going: 'Bitch, please, shut up and get the fuck out my face!' And Uncle Jove now slamming the egg turner down, put that half eaten bean burger into his gown pocket and raising fists, went: 'Ask and you shall receive! Act like a dumbness and you shall get knocked the fuck out, motherfucker! Yeah, dat's right, I'm the one and only true believer here, cos I believe Ima bout to get right up into yo asshole, but this time the gloves are coming off, yeah that's right - we about to get dirty.' Uncle Jove jogging on the spot, bouncing and bopping, fists flying, as giving them brachies an education, Uncle Jove fired at 'em again, spitting: 'Your Gaaad is nothing but a genie in a goddamn lamp, maan. And your religion? Well that ain't nothing but a sick ass programme created to enslave your motherfucking soul. All dem deities coming into existence only *under one condition*: that some fucking brain-dead monkey may come along and rub on that genie lamp—or open up that doom book (to unleash a thought form: a demon or god of the mind). Which just goes to show - all them supernatural beings never existed in the first place. It's all bullshit. It's all YOU. YOU are the one giving life to *dem tings* - it soley depends on you, which means it's all in your motherfucking head; see what I'm saying?'

Them two deacons now looking at Uncle Jove as if he'd just fucked their Momma in the asshole and slapped their daddy for watching. 'Ha, ha, ha. Look at your sorry asses. This here is the result of generational bad perception, bad intention and bad motherfucking belief—to the point you don't even know who the fuck you are. Tch! Maan, y'all gotta come up out of this bullshit, maan, and begin thinking for yo'selves; buncha stupid ass bitches.'

The deacons taken aback now, with one of them going:

'I'm gonna hafta ask you to stand down, sir, you're way outta line.'

Uncle Jove cocking an eyebrow, going: 'Well, what you gonna do about it, motherfucker? If you don't like it, I already told you what you can do with yo'self. So quit being a house bitch and do something about it, maan!'

Suddenly Uncle Jove snatched a bible out from under one of them deacon's arms, going: 'This here book, it is a myth, copied from a myth, copied from a myth that was stole off the ancient ancestors of the Golden Lands.'

Uncle Jove going to them boy: 'I mean, do you truly believe this shit in its current form. (Shaking the book in their faces) This is a fucking abomination.'

Them boys replying: 'Sir, we pledge our lives on that bible.'

Uncle Jove going: 'Damn, that is a shame. Y'all got some shit in your eyes and ears, maan, cos after all that I just got done telling you, if you still be thinking that this here book is the word of some Gaaad, then bitch, you more dumb than you look, and gotta wake the fuck up. This shit here in this here Bible, it all originated from the Golden Lands, maan, the Golden Lands. You might as well wipe your ass with this book, cos it's nothing but a straight up con job. Yeah, fact! When them imposters came along, dem bloodthirsty cave dwellers - they done stole the legacies, maaan, distorted the history and butchered the sacred stories of the ancient ancestors - changing the places and names and masquerading it all under a false narrative, purely for the sake of tricking dumb asses just like yo'selves, who, either got born or fell into it: the mind & soul trap that is "religion". A religion that dumbed down your consciousness in order to make y'all believe that Gaaad walked amongst us and suffered bowel moment and shat hisself. Shieet! I mean, come on, maan, that's like real simpleton shit. Just believing in that on its own is like being thrown under the spell of some cold, sick-ass, covert, psychological fuckery, right there. And the sad truth is that many brothas and sistas have fallen for it hook, line, and sinker.'

And just then, one of them deacons started shaking and convulsing—his religious foundation being challenged by the surge of fresh decree - to which he had no scriptural back-up *on hand* in order to discredit Uncle Jove's wild claims with. And so, doing what all brainwashed religious zombies do best, the lad began to fall back on his Jezem Jainko programming, commanding with venom; hand-to-sky: 'Father, in the name of Jezem, I plead the blood over this poor man's wretched soul. Right now Father, I plead the blood of Jezem over any entities who are trying to come against this poor man. I command a hedge of protection around him, that no weapon forged against him shall prosper—I thank-you Father for your mercy, may your will be done, in the loving name of Jezem, aaamen!' And while the lad was busy trying to deliver Uncle Jove, his counterpart, with head bowed, every now and then shouted out something like: "Yes, Father!" Or "Thank-you Jezem!" Or "Hallelujah!" Or "You are worthy Lord!" Or "Praise Jezem!"

And at the end of the deacon's tiraid, Uncle Jove was like:

'Yo! Shut the fuck up, maan. Don't you ever be doing that shit again—(looking to the counterpart) goddamnit, you lucky, son, I nearly ripped your fucking head off.'

The counterpart going: 'Jezem loves you, sir.'

Uncle Jove scoffing: 'Loves me, huh? Pfff, yeah, like the pope loves butt sniffing choirboys, I bet. Heck, you newbies know nothing, maan. And just by looking at you two, I'm willing to bet you dipshits have spent your entire lives talking to "Gaaad", am I right?'

Them deacons happily admitting that "Yes!" indeed they have. But Uncle Jove was unimpressed, going: 'Mmhmm. I guess I'd be right too in saying that not once has the motherfucker ever said "Hi" to you.' Them deacons as silent as the very god they talk to, as Uncle Jove now (coming round) ready to pack a DNA activating punch; spitting facts, went: 'Well then, going on your silence, it appears to me that you brachies have been talking to your motherfucking selves all this time. Ha! Ha! But y'all get what that is, dontcha? I mean, they just need to sniff a brotha sittin' in the corner talking to hisself, and already *BAM!* they got that shit on speed dial, bruh. In no time, ambulance crew at your exact location (all assembled) to straight-jacket-you-up - ready *to be* signed, sealed and delivered to the funny farm, you feel me?' Them boys looking at Uncle Jove as if he be tripping balls or sumthin'.

Uncle Jove cracking their heads with pure facts, breaking it down exactly in terms them deacons needed hearing—roaring and shaking that egg-turner in their faces, going: 'Y'all need to wake the fuck up, maan. I mean, in how many different ways do I gotta break it down for youse! And even if the days of the Drakazoid's witchcraft is all but over, y'all still need to be looking yourself square in the eye and accept yo'selves as chillens of the Sun. You need to erase their narrative from your consciousness and realize that you are Kings - the sovereigns of this realm; you know what I'm saying. Time to embrace the divinity within and elevate yo'self to the status of creator (lower case c). Now go! Go in peace and live brave lives!' And dropping his bible into the gutter—one of them deacon's received the coded message; his DNA activated—the download hitting the mark, as he got jump-started by the TRUTH—screaming down the road and tearing at his clothes like a bright-eyed madman, shedding decades of lies, self-deception and bondage—celebrating his new life; guilt-free, minus the shame and condemnation. Uncle Jove going: 'What a beautiful sight to behold. Now there's a free man.'

And still standing there in front of Uncle Jove, the deacon that was too much of a coward to think for himself, Uncle Jove handed him back his bible—saying: 'Here you go, son, it belongs in the trash—along with all them other Drakazoid lies. But you can only get to that realization once you overstand; the entire system is based upon a fiction. Now please, get off my land!"

Oh what a sight indeed—especially when beautiful people escape the clutches of dogma, religion, belief, and suppression. Yep. And all this tearing-up of misconception coming from our dear Uncle Jove... A discernible and awoke man, a guru master of sorts, a legend. And because of his thirst for knowledge and truth, I loved and respected Uncle Jove even more. For he broke it down in simple terms.

* * *

And when Uncle Lonnie was away in class with big ambitions of running his own auditing firm: a front for a big psychotropics lab; kept coolly under his wool flannel school cap—Ma Cookie would have her best friend, Aunt Bess, over (for company). Poor, emphysemic, fat-ankled Aunt Bess—a great but smelly lady, ugly as a witch's broom with big juicy moles on her face like fat poison berries; lethal enough to have massacred a small village. Her distracting wild fruits growing in amongst wiry wisps of silvery beard and tache-hair.

And in their self-knitted cardigans, pinned with cameo broaches, Ma Cookie and Aunt Bess would sit the day into cinders; window blinds pulled down, hunched over the kitchen table in the silhouette darkness—playing rounds of rummy, smoking Red Ruby's and sipping rum-strengthened tea, while on the stove supper cooked cosily, and on the fridge the FM faintly hummed radio theater, plus coffee and cigarette commercials.

And when it was just the three of us: Lonnie, Ma Cookie and me, we'd laugh to stitches-and-tears. Ma Cookie laughing so hard she'd fill-out red-faced. And we'd point and say: 'Check Ma out, she looks just like a wild turkey.' Uncle Lonnie and me rolling on the floor with Ma leaned up against the washer holding her stomach screaming 'Stop it!' The laughter and joy too much *that* none of us could breathe.

And these were amazing young times; innocent times—times way before my deep, dark weed and Amarantium-eating days—them lost days, when I held philosophy books as burdens, and blood and thunder poems as outlets—dreading too much and making no sense; a hormone imbalance the prognosis, coupled with the lack of essential nutrients, plus a worsening case of fossilized-turd syndrome. Though back then, not knowing much about nutrition; filled with toxins and vibing at the lower end of the energy spectrum, like an anxious fool, I placed blame on my poor heartbroken folks. This bust-up world, after all, their doing, hmm. Me being me; just another self-riddled, introspective teen with the shit of this world still ripe in my eyes, as I romanticized about death; trapped in my lower conscious mind, all self-absorbed and obsessed with masturbation, physical beauty, sex, pain and suicide—going around with losers, crazy people and troubled women.

And everyday, dropped off by the Seventh Seal Society Church school bus on Dawnlit Drive: a black stretch of asphalt that ran straight from Backwood's city center, to the outskirts of Sweet Place—I'd kick across the tall grass fields in my sad school shoes—scattering locusts and dandelion weeds as I passed through the great landscape of Saratoka Plains, home of El Morro Mountain, to spend time with Ma Cookie and Uncle Lonnie, until my dad knocked off from his shift at the fire brigade to fetch me in his '81 Ford Pickup: a poor, sad, beat-up little truck, that when at age-14 - learning to drive, instead of stabbing the breaks, I accelerated *SMACK!* straight into another vehicle. My parents having to dish out insurance for the damage to the guy's rear bumper. Our poor, sad Pickup never quite the same. The front right fender pushed back so far that the driver's door had to be prised open with a scraping metal on metal moan—every time my dad squeezed in and out of his crumpled chariot.

And Ma would spoil me rotten, making wholewheat toast plastered with cool marg, served with Vibrant Lotus tea and a side bowl of mixed sweet—while I'd be glued to my favorite TV show Danger Bay, when not found playing Spectravideo (SVI-738 MSX) games with Uncle Lonnie in the spare room that Ma named the 'Stink Room'. As all day, sitting in front of the monitor—sweating and farting; working that joystick—we'd play Beamrider and River Raid, Pitfall Harry, Manic Miner, Antarctic Adventure, Jack The Nipper, Commando and H.E.R.O.—slurping SodaStream through candy stripped straws—throwing more pureed farts up into the air. Yep, spoilt rotten, indeed.

And in Uncle Lonnie's backyard stood a haggard, termite infested Wendy house we named: 'The Lab'. A drafty, little nailed-up pile of planks, where all kinds of precious junk found on walks through Saratoka Plains, and digs through industrial and dead-end dumps, got stashed.

'The Lab' also became a neat little alchemists den, where under the watchful mentorship of Uncle Jove, we were instructed how to make monoatomic gold or what is also called

SARATOKA PLAINS

the Philosopher's Stone or Manna or Ormus: a magical element believed to restore one's original DNA structure; possibly even assisting in its evolution. A super nutrient reducing the need for consuming large qualities of food. Uncle Jove making the most legendary of potions. He was a wizard at it. All you needed was just a teaspoon, and a count to five to experience the greatest gunshot swig to the head. And everyone in the community used to partake of Uncle Jove's homebrew batch of *Quantum Zang!* the purest of manna known to kickstart the DNA and tingle the senses with a pure and undefiled *BUZZ!* that would jolt your pituitary gland into overdrive and release a swath of melatonin to ooze through your body like a jackpot of frothy molten lurve.

The popular phrase... *Take *Quantum Zang!* today and upgrade your DNA with a magical zap! ...somewhat of a jingle that floated around our community.

And yes, we ought to do our utmost to function at our best, through whole-food, low-fat, plant-based diets, along with maintaining elevated, positive emotions; keeping our avatars resonating at their optimum beneficial frequency. Afterall, what is our DNA, but a bio-organic antenna that is in constant communication with the Universe and the surrounding environment. Disrupt that signal and the Universe will hand you a mixed bag of goods. But fix the antenna; clearing up the signal—and now you've become a powerhouse of good intentions and beautiful dreams that are just itching to manifest.

'The Lab' also became a hideout where Uncle Lonnie and I performed experiments on his chemistry set. Uncle Lonnie, who, with an impressive collection of chemicals, all numbered in bottles with colorful labels, would cook-up experiments to turn copper coins into gold or the most impressive: "conjuring the black snake or sugar snake" which everyone loved to observe.

But first - in preparation: locking the flimsy, weather-buckled door - trapping the sound of termites gnawing and drawing the moth-bitten curtains; sealing the misery within, huddled around a Bunsen burner and a candle for illumination—

Uncle Lonnie and I would put our aprons, goggles and gloves on—ready to conduct patient, calculative experiments in the dark. And most times, waiting for Uncle Lonnie to prepare the ingredients or sometimes just day-dreaming and drifting off, while the chemicals took time to react—with chin resting on arms, peppering iron filings onto a candle flame, I'd watch, glow-faced, as vigorous sparks fizzed like dynamite ready to go *BANG!*

And of these infamous concoctions—the favorite was the sugar and saltpetre smoke bombs that we'd set alight on Dawnlit Drive—blanketing that strip of asphalt in thick white clouds of creamy smoke that forced drivers to slow down and *Baap!* hooters—shaking fists in the air as we ran off and hid—rolling in bursts of laughter in the bushes of the plains.

And we were so happy in them days. Every day - a practice in what we could get away with; without our parents finding out.

And Uncle Lonnie and I also made forts out on Saratoka Plains—recalling one in particular, built on top of Palveda Hill. We dug a massive hole—and covered it with a large piece of hardboard, leaving just a gap with branches of Mesquite leaf placed over that acted as the door. In the walls we gouged compartments for keeping fighting staves, spears and missiles: plastic bottles packed hard with moist sand, just in case a turf war kicked off—often imagining ourselves defending our fort from neighboring gangs. And our gang we named: the Moonrunners. A name we lifted off our favorite movie: The Warriors.

And in our neighborhood the two biggest gangs were the Screaming Skulls and the Valley Kings. And whenever we saw an affiliated gang member or a group of them, it would seem like something out of a movie, as if they weren't real, standing there so notorious and cool; feared rebels that were to be stared at in wonder and facination - wiry characters on a blade's edge— exuding so much poise that to speak to them would only blow the mystery.

And often at Mini Cini; our local cinema, gang members would hang out donned in denim jackets: covered in patch badges; jeans ripped, as sprawled over chairs and throwing popcorn at one another, they looked so dangerous and eternal with a girl on each arm. And as a kid you couldn't help but be attracted through a type of hero worship of these bad boys. And one girl, whose boyfriend was a member of the Screaming Skulls, I had a huge crush on her. Her name, Kim. She lived next door to Léguvan and I loved her. She was beautiful, blonde, blue-eyed and juicy. And I imagined her being my girlfriend (so bad) that I had dreams of us together—holding hands and snogging. But she was ten years older than me, and knew things about boys which probably would have made me sick with seizures of premature ejaculation—cos at my young age it was more than enough to look up girls skirts. And for this I kept a special journal. Day-by-day making entries in neat rows and columns of all the girls I liked and the color of their panties. And some girls wore the same panties for weeks and smelt of sandwich spread and sweat. And normally these were the tomboys who could beat any boy at arm wrestles and dashes.

Now the Screaming Skulls and the Valley Kings were each at least thirty members strong—armed with bats, chains, sticks, knives - you name it. Recalling one sunny day on the Saratoka Plains: Uncle Lonnie and I somehow found ourselves right in the middle of a pow-wow *between* these two gangs, when all of a sudden, chaos. Something must have been said between the two leaders, cos in no time - swear words were being exchanged, a punch landed, and then *Bingo!* - a proper gang brawl. The whole lot of 'em piling into one another as fists flew, weapons were wielded, heads got clobbered and skin marked. It was a dust cloud of mayhem, when suddenly, we found ourselves swooped up with a fraction of the Screaming Skulls, fleeing the Valley Kings—boys on the run boasting battle scars in celebration of this momentous event. And all of it was so exciting and happening so fast *we* didn't know who we were. But for the moment we were uninitiated gang members of the Screaming Skulls. One boy proudly pointing to a bloody stab wound in his Achilles where a Valley Kings gang member had chucked him with a flick knife.

And so fleeing with our tails partially wagging between our legs, we childishly imagined the worst—for these were only boy gangs and not the serious hard-livings, bad, drug and gun gangs like the infamous Bárbaro Incas or the Māratopia Syndicate. For no one ever got killed or badly hurt by these encounters - and walked away with only cuts and bruises, as snapping through bush and branches we giggled in our escape. And it was Uncle Lonnie and I that led that small party of the Screaming Skulls to safety—all the way to our secret hiding spot.

Then one boy, piggybacking his little brother, shouted: 'Caleb! Aah, no!'—shrugging off Caleb who landed on his bum and began to cry. Everyone "shushing" Caleb - but cracking sniggers when they saw that Caleb had peed all the way down his brother's back. Poor Caleb sprinkling tears and staring big bush baby eyes at everyone as he trembled like a moth. Every little sound making him snivel and hiccup "heartsore-sobs" for his "Momma" - as now keeping still with heads hung low; digging sticks into the sand, everyone waited for Caleb to stop being such a baby. And by the time Caleb died down it was time to go home. The Valley Kings CLEVER—probably already with their families all dressed in pajamas (after bath time); eating supper in front of the TV, while we foolish ones; still in hiding—watched as the soft day *now* got beaten black and blue by the burly thick night that treacled over our heads like intoxicated blood. The chirruping of crickets and the clicking of frogs bristling in sync with the watery lights that shimmered in the pinned-up distance that back-dropped Saratoka Plains.

And often during the day, little friends like frogs and toads would pay visits to our fort—seeking the moist shade it provided in the hot-zinging Cicada heat, while in class, staring out the window comatose, I'd be somewhere else, wondering if I was actually just dreaming - lost in la-la land, while Uncle Lonnie - still fresh and good in class, was raising his hand to all his teacher's questions—passing tests with merit. And when the last school bell rang, it was time, and we'd be back in Saratoka Plains again, atop of Palveda Hill. And on such a day— pulling away the dry Mesquite branches, we got the biggest scare of our lives and stood there frozen—bracing ourselves like good little boys, holding our breath at the sight of a fully-grown Western Redjewel; more than 4ft long, as it undulated in s-shape movements - going snakey, snakey out from our fort; just millimeters from our feet. And the both of us like pilgrims tied to totem poles; preparing to get ripped from their mortal shells, we were terrified, and ended up muttering the mumbles of the ancients; incantations of pure soul, as almost appearing in slow-mo, we watched as that serpent took ages; its polished tongue darting out like a slippery forked-vein, filled with slow, black, bubbling bile.

Another encounter with the infamous Western Redjewel was while spring-cleaning the garage. And beneath some dusty cobwebs I spotted a juvenile coiled up in the corner. And immediately ran into the house and rang up Uncle Lonnie to come over. And by the time Uncle Lonnie arrived, my daddy and I had already caught the little fella in a big 5-liter glass jar. And so, deep into the Saratoka Plains we marched, ready to set our baby Redjewel free. But just as Uncle Lonnie took that little fella out, the bugger struck him on the forefinger - juveniles naturally more aggressive than adults - their bite as potent as the Kaukas Krucifyre - certainly something to teach one a thing or two about a harrowing death. For when that neurotoxin gets into your system, within 30 min, you'll not only find it difficult to breathe, but PYREXIA: a fire fever will take hold—a literal hell, as searing through your body, boiling your blood, you'll be burning up from the inside. And without an antiserum you'll be as dead as a doornail within two to five hours. But luckily for Uncle Lonnie, he had on my daddy's heavy-duty work gloves. But nevertheless, we sure caught a wake-up, and respectfully released that vicious little blighter into the rabbit-tail grass... Where it disappeared—snaking off into Saratoka Plains with a cat-like hiss.

9.

ZEKE MORRY

FINALLY I made it back home. Our house the only bungalow with its porch light still on—shedding a warm nicotine glow over the velvet pelts of the puma-like geckos that skittered up and down the sides of the house - as they chased moths and mosquitoes.

Stomping mud onto the rubber porch mat, I unlaced my boots, slipped the key into the door and stepped inside—greeting my mother, Zöe Snakes: a woman tough as batons and as sweet as coconut ice. A sometimes daft lady who'd ask questions like: 'Where do all the birds go when they die?' or 'Where do flies sleep at night?'—Yes, mother-dear-mother, now curled up on the sofa doing crosswords, while father-dear-father was in bed wrestling the snores.

* * *

It was late by the time I got indoors. Most people already asleep or winding down, preparing for Monday and the "back-to-work blues".

I kissed my mother good night and drifted off to my room, closing the door behind with a tickled sigh.

I struck a sputtering match, lit the candle at my bedside, and sat hunched in the semi-darkness; face flickering, as beyond the ash-dump bottles on my windowsill, I gazed into the chromium night. Shadows danced across the ceiling and upon the walls in adherence to the flame, as it bobbed up and down—swirling *tinges* of aquamarine, cobalt blue, amber, reddish-brown, pale-yellow, light-green and emerald *wavelenghts* - a luminescence that slipped over the glowing bottles like oil slick over a crisp dew drop.

My interest in vintage *glass* bottles began on an ash-dump dig in Saratoka Plains, with my good ole buddy Zeke Moray, who for me was both thee Desert and Mountain Man rolled into one fine cig. And just like these "cigarette heroes" of the wilderness adventure, with tough leather faces like tanned old boots, and eyes forever squinting coolly into the sun—Zeke appreciated a good smoke, while buzzing legendary thoughts about his place in time.

    I made friends with Zeke Moray during my two years at Shiprock High, 1990-1992 - a trial of errors I simply couldn't fathom—falling out of desks from sheer boredom. The whole prison-style system of speak when you're spoken to, and having to raise your hand to ask permission to take a piss, I hated it. It was fucking nightmare. Especially anything to do with sums. Recalling my parents, 2 years earlier—holding hope, as they carted me every Sunday to visit the renowned Mrs Evelyn Andersen's residence; for private maths tuition. Mrs Evelyn Andersen, a Cheyneecian from the Northern District—with a perm and a goatee - who wore big retro specs and tried her outrageous best to hammer algebra and mumbo jumbo sums into my fogged out brain. Yeah, poor Mrs Andersen, an enthusiastic, sufferable woman, who managed only to advance me in "matters of perversion" - as pinning down a cool nerve—I'd take snapshots with my mind's eye of Evelyn's huge, tanned bangers—nodding away while she mouthed "whatevers"—as all I could envision was sweet Evelyn gobbling my cock with that filthy beak of hers - crammed swollen with a parched tongue that could lick the skin off a sausage. Yes. That was it as far as sums were concerned. Good head. Job done.

ZEKE MORRY

Then after about a month, Mrs Andersen got pretty brassy; slightly off key in fact—purposefully letting her juggers hang loose—leaning over me, braless in low cut dresses—as now in that house it would be just the three of us. Her old man: mister invisible—knocking about in the back room as bald as a billiard ball, bound to his electric wheelchair. That poor doomed man paralyzed from the neck down - minus hands - all because he molested a 7-year old girl, whose daddy just happened to be an old-time fixer. The event part of a grim history. A time of small-town livings and darkened rooms with curtains drawn; all the way across the border over in *lonely* Cheyneecia, in the town of Huckle. And all the townsfolk were aware of "the molestation". He being a sick man. But as all small communities get healed through the power of gossip and righteous justice, when that girl's daddy found out about Mr Andersen's transgression, he swore he'd break Mr Andersen in two - a shocking event that was never spoken of ever again in the town of Huckle. The incident taking place on a night like any night *with suspense and impending doom in the air*—as racing over to the tavern Mr Andersen frequented - that girl's daddy BURST IN - everyone turning around *almost in rehearsed expectation*. And as that girl's daddy stood in the entrance, bearing a power drill - everyone stared breathless—until breaking the spell - he strolled over and addressed Mr Andersen, going: 'Weathering the storm, are you?' To which Mr Andersen, sheepishly looking up while closing his eyes, knodded with a big dumb ass grin on his face.

And with Mr Andersen seated there at his favorite spot, one pint down; in celebration of his sad shitty life—that girl's daddy, stepping over, grabbed Mr Andersen by the shoulder and drilled that filthy child molester through both his kneecaps. And when Mr Andersen let out a blood curdling scream - somebody in the backroom went 'Shhht..!' Nobody in the tavern lifting a finger. For it was as if what was to come had already been sanctioned. And then that girl's daddy bought Mr Andersen a double shot of bourbon for being such a good sport and all. And being only a few minutes into the game, Mr Andersen was already close to tapping out. But that girl's daddy insisted that Mr Andersen honor the free round—snarling between gritted teeth: 'Punish it. It'll take the edge off what is to come.' And Mr Andersen, when he heard the steel in that girl's daddy's voice, he nearly puked up all over himself - reeling like motherfucker trapped in an axe murderer's wet dream; a sickening sensation gripping him, for judgment day had arrived, as with eyes closed; tearful, Mr Andersen slugged back that double-shot (gagging). That girl's daddy applauding Mr Andersen's willingness to take his lesson to the next level - a slow menacing clap gripping everyone in the tavern, as that girl's daddy went: 'Ooo, the power of posi-ti-vi-ty. I just love positive people, I bet you do to, huh?' firmly slapping Mr Andersen on the back. The whole tavern silent as snooker match—all eyes focused on the winning shot. And what now seemed to take ages for Mr Andersen, finally had arrived. The moment of ugly truth and beautiful justice. As that girl's daddy, a bit fidgety; his rage building, with a clear mind and calm certainty, took that powerdrill once again and drilled Mr Andersen in his groin, seven times - pulverising his private parts—making *certain* he'd be fucked for good. And then to anoint the occasion - that girl's daddy bought Mr Andersen a pink mojo cocktail in celebration of him loosing his virginity to a powerdrill. 'Don't wimp out on me now, boy, believe me, you want to be fully coherent for your next bit of fun.' That girl's daddy patting Mr Andersen on the shoulder, giving it a squeeze, going: 'Not long to go now, son, not long to go.'—as sat opposite him—staring right through him—he waited anxiously for Mr Andersen to sip his drink. And then, as the last drop of lemonade and rum rolled down Mr Andersen's throat, that girl's daddy went: 'Well, guess it's about time then, ain't it.' And in hearing that, Mr Andersen froze, realising things were about to get way more fucked up than he ever could have imagined. And that girl's daddy stood up, took a barstool, and with it bashed Mr Andersen right at the base of the neck, snapping it, crippling him for life. And while Mr Andersen lay there unconscious, that girl's daddy, going a bit too far, hacked off Mr Andersen's hands with a "kukri" knife concealed under his jacket (strapped to his body). And reaching round, unhooking a blowtorch from his tool belt, he lit it and proceeded to cauterise the bloody stumps. And then, the *pièce de résistance*—the icing on the cake: as that girl's daddy unbuckling his trousers, squatted down, releasing his bowels all over Mr Andersen's head - all for the hurt Mr Andersen *had laid* upon his little princess. And everyone in the tavern knew it had to be done. And when the lawman and his deputies came sniffin' around smellin' of sweat, leather, shoe shine and chew tobacco—everyone stuck to the same story: "Didn't see a goddamn thing, officer."—stating they all ran outside to witness a fantastic anomaly in the sky. And when they returned to the tavern, Mr Andersen was already on the floor - hands all chopped off - head coated in shit.

And so, being a good boy, I kept my hands all to myself. I mean, who was I to touch a marked man's woman.

But then one day, Mrs Andersen caught me twisting my knob through a special hole in my pocket. And slapping away my hand she shook her head—unzipping my fly—going: 'Tch, tch, tch, tch, you should know better, boy.'—as sliding her nails into the slit of my pants, grabbing the base of my cock—she began stroking me while drooling long lines of spit she sucked back and swallowed with lust. And from the backroom, I then started to hear these rousing, knocking sounds. "Shit!" I thought - could this be the man himself. Mr Andersen I guess having woken up from his post midday nap, now ready for his side order of sea-juice.

Then, as if a switch had been flipped—everything went into friggin' overdrive. For when I moaned, that bitch Mr Andersen moaned. His moan though, weird... Like that of a man in distress; a withering, sick moan sinister as fuck. And regardless that Mr Andersen was the loser of all losers, I had to hand it to him, the fool was bang on point, like he had *that shit* down pat - growing louder like some mad, mystical bitch in the start-up of a thrashing orgasm—cos with each of my expressions of delight, which only encouraged Mrs Andersen to jerk me off even harder, Mr Andersen got louder and louder. And then taking it as far as I could—hitting my verge—holding on for dear life: my barrel cocked hard with two hot solid cartridges of throbbing jism; burning to be blasted out - riding my moans; layered just beneath my joy—I could hear Mr Andersen in the backroom rattling convulsions - flat out in hot pursuit of my bubbling climax. Mr Andersen, so excited, I feared he was gonna dislocate his body and injure himself. The electric wheelchair: his "Glide Machine", making complicated whirring sounds as it waltzed him across the room and banged him into the walls. Mr Andersen making noises so vigorous, I thought he had gone into some kind of uncontrollable spine-snapping fit, as then rudely, without warning—in the ensuing madness of that explosive moment—taking me by surprise, Mrs Andersen drew out her wrinkled teat, and squeezing it, squirted rancid milk 'Psssss' straight into my mouth. Blergh! Her menopausal curd souring my face to the point that while *still* in the process of pulling a sweeter expression (my balls on overload alert), hit between these two intense sensations (the sweet & the sour), my face contorted like a man in agony, as I succumbed, ejaculating all over her rotted tit.

Then, as soon as the rush of wind in my blood; whizzing in my ears, calmed down, I heared from the backroom heavy panting, as with a smile of accomplishment, Mrs Andersen led me by the hand down a long corridor and into a dark room. And there he was - in full bloom - a sack of shit with a creepy smile on his fucked up mug. The embodiment of "Payment for Poor Life Choices". The instant bitch-slap of karma with a face, as then, like a mother bird with a cropful of regurgitated shit—straddling her husband, Mrs Andersen hugged her old man's sorry head - who with tears of gratitude - licked my cum off his wife's banged-up tit.

And that did it for me. Blew my brains way out like firecracker dust lighting up a night sky in celebration of nothing. I mean, is freewill really worth it if it's going to lead one into a state of high entropy. And yeah, of course, I could have gone along with it all, but then what next: eating his wife's shit off my cock? No way, maan! These dirty fuckers were certainly on another level on the Richter Scale of seismic disorder. And besides, at age 15, shit like that was not high on my bucket list - more like my "Fuck that!" list. So rather than endure that weird plow-run into the straits of defilement; being supportive of Mr Andersen's "Menu Wish List" of hot nutriet all sorts—I decided to jump that particular "delivery train" and told my folks, 'Hey! I won't be needing those shit sums anymore.' And when they asked me why, I answered:

'Why the fuck not!'

This turn of fate ultimately the catalyst that got me into reading. My love of stories-told, stemming from one bold incident. And so I guess in a way I must thank you, Evelyn—I will always hold your "bangers" in high regard.

* * *

And when I got into public school, the place I met Zeke; "Thrown to the wolves", as my mother put it—afraid her sweet hatchling would be corrupted by "children of the world"—in my second year, already I had developed a leather gut for Rolling Head vodka—licking swigs off my cool drink bottle behind the tennis courts; hidden in the bushes—smoking cigs and turning green—chucking-up lungs—carrying the party on into class—blazing my brains out on Tippex thinners—sat back of the class—sucking solvents off my tie, which by the year's end was covered with white splotches.

And already then I knew I was bad, and that it was all too late, losing grip. For all I wanted was to write poems and dream and experiment with life, like some badass legend 19th-century poet with a taste for whores, hash, absinthe, red wine, coffee and sublime cigars.

Now my first impression of Zeke, in them early days, was BOY-ADVENTURER—he being like some heroic character straight out of an adventure dime novel. Zeke, after all, thee fishing champ of the Western Region, and youngest person ever to receive territorial colors for fresh and saltwater fishing—bunking school every week just to journey up the West Coast—surviving on nothing but Old Beast sherry, cigarettes, weed, and catch of the day. And if not on the misty crashing coastline, Zeke would be found roughing it in the rugged Elcassa Badlands—surrounded by scorpions, snakes, and spiders with only his wits and that thick buffalo-hide nape of his to keep him alive. And often after such long hauls of solitude and soul-searching beleaguerment, Zeke would come back with true vibes from "Ma Nature", as all abuzz—stinging wisdoms of flight and insightful parable, he'd bellow:

'Look all around you Freddy ... you can't deny it ... the universe, look-at-her ... she's like one big fucking vagina, maaan; and sheez lookin' at you ... begging for it, boyeee—so go ahead, ride that beautiful queen off into the sunset—cos I tell you, maaan ... no man should ever be hung up swearing apology ... for life ain't no apology, maaan ... it's your crowning glory, so take it by the hips and fuck that bullseye, boyeee!'

And like the survivor of some lost gypsy race, I considered Zeke to be from an earlier time, like some golden relic or priceless token the gods had left behind. And Zeke said that if ever he had to "Check Out", he'd go out like Van Gogh, and shoot himself in the heart. But he'd do it in the desert, cos Zeke feared wheat fields—saying there was something too religious about them. And that's the way he'd go—death from heartache and

ZEKE MORRY

pain of life. Blasted off this godforsaken rock. *BAM!!* Gone solid like some a god-star shot to the other side of nowhere. Yep, that was Zeke all the way. A rough man, true to the bone.

And during my infancy, I recall a certain voice that haunted me. And only when Zeke handed me a cassette tape of The Greatest Hits, by a band named The Doors, did I finally put a name to the voice. In fact, only when I listened to the last track, did all the hovering-blue-terrifying-intense mystery hit home. That voice being the same "ghost" which echoed through the sparsely furnished flat my parents rented, in Pelmoda, not far from Auburn Hills; as a young married couple. My dad crazy on this one tune—playing that damn "Riders On The Storm" 7-single over and over—non-stop. And that was all I heard. Nothing else but the crash of thunder and rain and the tinkly piano and that voice, the voice of Jim Morrison—over and over, from the time I was kicking lengths in my mother's womb juice, right up until I was pooing in towel nappies—lying on my back and staring up at the ceiling - wondering when it was all going to stop.

And out of life, Zeke's three most beloved things were: fishing, snakes, and Jimmy Page. And through Zeke's idol worship of the legendary axe man, enthusiastically, the Zekester sticky-tacked his daddy's entire Led Zeppelin LP collection (the vinyls inside) to his bedroom wall. Them 12-inch records still unbelievably intact, considering Zeke and his older brother Robin, as little rascals, used to Frisbee them around the backyard.

And Zeke named Physical Graffiti his all-time favorite album. Kashmir and Ten Years Gone his top two songs. Zeke, adamant, that Ten Years Gone must be played at his funeral— BLASTED! over the boat's PA, while his corpse; trawling the brine, got mauled by sharks and nibbled at by fish, turtles, and gulls.

And armed with only a bow and arrow, Zeke would hunt guinea fowl and quail on the Saratoka Plains. Plucking them pink

and goosy-fleshed - only to roast them crudely over a fire; sat cross-legged like a true meditative bush-worn scout, devouring his hunt—ripping flesh clean off bone like a real little savage.
And ever since Zeke was 12, he held an affinity for smoking— eating through packs of cigarettes as if they were love-on-fire. All that rich nicotine and tar earning him a deep gravel voice— making Zeke sound way beyond his years, likened to that of an eccentric, sackcloth sage, hailed from crashing coastline to howling desert.

And Zeke was also a notorious excessive walker—thighs built like stallions that bulged through tight jeans, as over the great sand trails of the Western Region—wearing his red polished boots with tire tread soles—Zeke would stride from shore to shore, desert to desert—entering realms unknown to man, bound in otherworldly states of mind; his soul so gone you could almost call it: statuesque. Yep, Zeke, truly was 'The Man'.

And often on visits to Zeke's home, I'd enjoy his room— browsing Zeke's fascinating realm: all the objects collected on his boyhood adventures. Stuff like bird skulls and eagle eggs, and hawk feathers, boar tusks, including artefacts such as flint arrowheads, and egg shell necklace beads (made by natives of the land). And of course Zeke also had an impressive collection of vintage glass bottles, along with a huge scratch of cowry shells— plus the largest hoard of fossilized shark teeth: Carcharodon megalodons, all found on Zeke's "beachcomber walks" along the Western Region's coastline.

Zeke also kept a large fish tank in his bedroom, that contained snakes he caught on Saratoka Plains, or on Shiprock Golf Course; bare handed no less. Zeke's hands as hard and swollen as leather mitts cured in brine; bucketed from the roughest known seas to have crashed on rugged rock.

And Zeke also dug his "weed", big time proportions of a "connoisseurship-like" infatuation, as with eyes closed, hands behind head—leaned back, feet up—Zeke would chill with

ZEKE MORRY

goose bumps all over his body, as he shivered in absorbtion of the truesome sound of Luciano Pavarotti—who he visualized as one giant formidable lung. For in Zeke's mind, Pavo was absolutely thee all time grand swooning lung of the opera show. The ultimate swan song hero.

And sometimes the two of us we'd spend the whole day smoking up a large biscuit tin of weed, collapsed in the baking sun—lying amongst beach brambles, beneath a titling viridian sky; so stoned we'd be unable to walk, talk or even roll another fattie.

And all that weed I grew myself. Plants 6ft tall. I had so much, I couldn't smoke it fast enough, and was literally giving the shit away—stuffin' heads and leaves into grip seal coin bags (them ones banks use)—just to quell the bulk-harvest ten man-sized plants produced.

And yesss, it was strange weed, I must admit. Spumes of mind-blow that would rangle and tangle your soul. A fine smoke; voodoo-dragged hot of the cherry and devoured like lurve on fire. A fine smoke that would stick in your throat like cactus fangs, as coughing up in vain - too late - that snake-like potion already would be pumping through your arteries—boiling your brain and cooking it up like some sacrificial side of meat in a juju doctor's jungle-pot. I mean; "Fuck Yeah!!" that 'mule' sure could kick (some) - giving you a head-buzz that would render you so 'tombstoned' you'd be earthing like a jelly-kneed, first-time believer: skull all weighed up and shit - heavy with dreams and sorcery and hot-confusion *tantamount*—along with dizzy cantations; bare babblings, enough to make even the holiest of monks seem barbaric. Yep. A real brain-buster that homegrown 'kick'.

And once again, I recall, latched onto that 'mule', as Zeke and I found ourselves (on a gusty winter's night) zipped-up in a red and white (vertical striped) beach tent, that I had been living in (going on two months) in my parents backyard.

And so there we were; the whole night—blazing away, minds nailed down like jello to a back-alley wall (them real infested places), them dark and dodgy locales *whereby* down the track, far as the eye can tell, a trail of used condoms, beer caps, Nitrope pipes, burnt matches, glass tubes, weed bags, ciggie butts, foil cones, used-up rolling paper booklets, bottles, paper snails, and roaches litter the scene like shiny kiddy toys scattered across the living room floor of some desolate rundown home for junkies and dexotrine-heads.

And after about an hour of chatting, our minds clicked into "timelessness mode", in which we began staring at a candle made of crayon. The whole tent smelling of Crayola. And we must have been there hours, just staring at some glitter dancing around in a pool of wax at the base of the wick, when all of a sudden, Zeke was on top of me - strangling me like a red-faced nut. And for a long time I couldn't understand why he did that. But 18-years-later (at age 40) I put it to him, and he reminded me: 'Don't you remember, you dumb fuck, you almost set the tent on fire.' A moment of blankness, indeed—the first time ever having lost myself completely to another side of "me". Cos from then on, everything kinda slipped *in-and-out* dimensionally—as I began to wander through life like some bleedin' heart broke head, all spaced out and sore; swallowed up in devils and darkness forever.

And yeah, that weed; for sure, was pretty badass. And sometimes I'd be just staring at one spot—having to remind myself: 'Breathe, you sonofabitch.' A love and hate relationship; my romance with the weed. And for a time, she, that weed-Queen, held me under the bridge, until I ended up so paranoid, I began cooking up all kindsa conspiracies, that even the birds on rooftops and in trees were spies, alerting the people of my arrival into town - all for the big preperation of the "scene" and so forth. Yep, I was the guy the entire neighborhood feared. People increasing their walking pace, just to get past my house. The heavy magnetic energy from my conjurings tugging on 'em; wanting to swallow their souls whole, I guess.

And so like this it was I who was the grotty troll, hunched in the shadows like a king of filth and incantations—the deep hole I had crawled into, a creative cave that stimulated my artistic juices—recalling sitting up nights to work on a huge collage made of porn mag and Vogue cut-outs. My soundtrack to the project, back-to-back: US3's "Broadway & 52nd" and Deep Forest—as carrying well on into the darkest hour; just before dawn, I'd catch the sounds of poor folk rising for work. Their noise, a sign for me to down tools and creep beneath the covers to catch up on some more cool, lavish dreams.

* * *

And Zeke's household—a homely cat manor—housed at least twelve cats. All kinds of jungle striped, eagle-faced, owl looking, mousey, snake-eyed, Buddha-type creatures with dove-like cooings—all murr-murr-murring on their sacred spots like little meditative statuettes, either indoors or outside in shrubs or on the garage roof (shaded by a tall pine) or beneath the fruit trees—where chameleons spent their days darting snotty tongues into the hovering haze of fruit-flies and midges; attracted by the warm fermenting fruit.

And other than being a man of nature, Zeke was the town's star of note—a dance floor champ, which naturally translated into him being a groover in the sack. His lovely drilling-dick dripping fever juice—hence, the dance floor *being* the only pick-up-line Zeke needed—GIRLS chanting his name as he partied-it-up "Elephantine" like the original shirtless brute. For in them days, Zeke was hailed "Catalyst" of the rave and dance scene in Backwood. It being his rebirth spectre: the adult rising from the dead skin of the child snake.

And Zeke would sneak Xycamorphinol pills (wrapped in foil), into nightclubs, hidden under his foreskin—fooling bouncers who'd conduct searches (semi-thorough) the anus and groin a big no-no probing zone, as they took drugs off the not-so-wise patrons who'd conceal whatever "drug of choice" in their socks or pockets or wallet or hoodie - only for the bouncers to pop whatever drug they confiscated, who later-on would be seen outside the club - locked into the music and doing their own robotic dance moves like workers, bored, after having done all the main labor; and are now only killing time.

And when Zeke hit the dance floor—BABY, did he own it. As "man alive!" everybody would stop and form a circle around Zeke, just to watch this "man of the moment", with top off, cig in mouth—doing his stuff. A real "rough-round-the-edges" man, ole Zeke, with cool dance moves that would inspire everyone to just lose it. That rhapsodic signature bod of his with well-shaped pecs, six-pack abs, tanned skin and clean dripping sweat, famous and innocuous. Yesss, nothing else to say, but sigh: 'Zeke'. For everyone, part of the hard-core drug and dance scene, during '96-'98, Backwood, wanted to party it up with The Man. Zeke's star-like reputation earning him blowjobs in toilet cubicles, along with hazy cool sexual endeavours in Jacuzzis at after parties. Even proposals of marriage—GIRLS throwing themselves at him, all dressed-up, barely clothed, just for Zeke— queuing outside clubs just to get a peek or to be near him; to hug a bicep or to ultimately fuck "The Wild Man of Backwood".

And years earlier now, one night in '91—hopelessly sozzled and stoned—washed-out and clunkered—turkeyed sideways like a punch-drunk virgin after a one-rounder with a battle-scarred whore, I got buddy hugged into a corner between two grinning boys: Kong and Bong, all tanned-up and sharp with surfer cuts, who fed me hard shots of fire-wine—poking a dope-filled ciggie into my mouth and lighting it—to which I ended up totally 'Cheeched'—barely able to walk myself home: three steps forward, only to fly back two - spread on the ground in fits of laughter. And each time, a growling Zeke had to drag me to my feet. But after several falls, he got fed up and socked me a good one on the ear *POW!*—my eyeball jumping and my back teeth chattering; struck with the force of Zeke's solid mitt, as tweeting stars and little planets twirled my spinning head.

And figuring myself sober—I convinced Zeke I was cool enough to drag-heel-it home. And with a concerned: 'Okay, your funeral.' Zeke gave me the hawk eye as we split ways. My head still zinging as I headed up Dawnlit Drive, when all of a sudden, staggering along that blacktop, my legs caved in *and next thing I knew* I was sprawled out across that motor swash; cheek pressed to the tarmac - staring dead ahead at a huge truck gunning toward me like a looming beast. And all I can recall was this rush-of-bliss that washed over me, ready for that big mean contraption to deliver me straight into the arms of my next incarnation. And it's not like I had a choice; couldn't move a muscle, as the blindening headlights zoomed larger *on that* rumbling heap of shimmering chrome ready to plow right through meat, sinew and bone, when unexpectedly from nowhere, just in time, I felt a strong determined tug on my arm—dragging me from the destined path of that sky high juggernaut. It was Zeke.

As it turned out, after we separated, good ole Zeke kept eyes on me all that time, aware that I just might fall. For just as that big metal bastard was nearly on top of me, Zeke Moray, my 'Guardian'—snatched me from certain death—saving me—and preventing me from being obliterated at the feel-good, dumb age of 17.

18.

JOHNNY SNAKES

MY room was small and cozy—and in one corner crouched an antique fold-down writing desk, inherited from my granddaddy Johnny Snakes, who wore a big eagle tattoo on his chest; a chain between its talons, with two great big balls: "Atlas globes" each-end, that swayed with real heft. And in a way that tattoo represented Johnny Snakes—whose soul soared through life unconcerned. Johnny Snakes, an eagle spirit in every sense, who took life by the balls.

And Johnny Snakes, life and joy of our family, would entertain us on harmonica, bamboo flute, and electric organ; all self-taught, but was especially loved on Brazilian six string, often joking: "And now for an ex-Beatle song."—and then he'd be off—flying somewhere; head tripping, twanging and strumming his beloved - singing the mantras of the great shamen, eyes closed, as he blew his brains in a sunlit dream—vibes uplifting, as we all: eagle-faced and in a trance; hearts buzzing rhapsodic, flew away on our spirit journey - guided by our elder tribesman, our guru freak, our Alpha rock. Our tight knit tribe safe under the wing of good ole granddaddy Johnny Snakes.

And it was Johnny Snakes' wife, Ricky Snakes' mom, my soft-spoken, violet-eyed gran—who on Yellowwood Road, Backwood, ran a hostel for abused and troubled women. Granny Snakes, who, as big Mother Goose *to all these girls*—cared for each one of them as her own. A poor, selfless woman—who even after she retired from her position as Hostel Matron, was visited by the girls, who called her Ma and gifted her with cakes, tarts and knitted things like slippers and crocheted toilet roll covers; all bought from the flea market down at the Grand Parade.

And often at the Hostel I'd sleepover in the ground floor living quarters where Granny and Johnny Snakes resided—recalling a little taxidermy mountain goat on the mantelpiece that stood staring with big-scary-bug eyes. Its frightening face illuminated by a street lamp that beamed into the spare room window. A ghastly little figure that imposed insomnia upon me, as literally it felt like its eyeballs were burning into the back of my neck—all-night-long. And I recall the eerie bathroom: its full pedestal, Art Deco handbasin with Victorian taps that drip-echoed in the dank semi-darkness that smelt of Savlon, shaving cream; and the soap-on-a-rope that hung from a wall-mounted shut-off valve; next to a rusting electric-fired geyser, that spat and sputtered above a bath with an orange water stain that ran into a slurping, glug-bound plug hole. And most times (back of the bathroom) on a toilet with a long flush-chain attached to a high-level cistern I'd spend "ages" just reading War and Battle Picture Library comics, keeping an eye on the big daddy long-legs above me—jiggling on a web, while at the same time I read, and observed, and learned.

And barefoot without fail, I'd always manage to step-cold into a damp patch sprinkled with carpet freshener. A particular longhaired rug the "designated target" for my grandparents' dog, Sintu, to shit or throw up on. And on the rare occasion my grandparents would catch that little bug-eye chomping its own turds, shouting: 'Sintu! No! Bad dog!'—causing that little shit-biter to scamper off with a steaming ripe turd in its mouth. My grandfather throwing it with a slipper as it yelped; skulking away to hastily chew down on turd meat, hidden under an old ball-and-claw sofa in the spare room—only to appear later, meekly trying to lick everyone on the face with its turd-breath.

And three times a day, every day, Granny Snakes would play a ding-dong tune on the dinner chime—calling all the girls into a big hall where food was served, hot out the pot. And in one corner stood an upright piano beside a performance stage—whereby, every December 25th, in celebration of the best of days;

midwinter, as well as the celebration of Spring: the resurrection: the recycling of seasons and stars in April, dismal plays were put on. Most of these girls on psychiatric meds suffering depression or some kind of mental breakdown. The performances put on as a kind of sad yearning for the childhood they never knew. And during such grim festivities REALITY was made even sadder for these girls, who still (but not unless you were told) had parents. Parents who never showed up once to see their child perform - an act of kindness that may have stoked a glimmer of joy in the heart; even for just a couple of hours of make believe.

And so, to the sound of that four-note dinner chime, the girls would sail down the stairwells. And sometimes being bad, I'd bash the dinner chime an hour before the cooks were ready to serve. And some not so bright girls would come down, and there I'd be standing with the sounding mallet in one hand, and sucking the thumb off the other, feeling bad. Some of these girls victims of abuse. Some born with broken hearts, while others were just broken.

And one of the girls: a stout, short-haired, snub-nosed, blue-eyed, bull dyke called Gary; lovely as homemade mede—with chin stubble and a teardrop tattoo on her face; MISTRUSTIVE of men, saying they made her feel weird in her skin; harder than jail bars, spent 3 years in a juvenile detention center for slashing the throat of her drunken dad, who began molesting her after his wife withered away; bitten by a cancer bug.

And Gary loved me true, something to do with having a good energy. And she'd often offer me solid heads-up advice, such as: 'Now remember Freddy, don't take sweeties from strange uncles, you hear me now ... them dirty old fools will kill your dreams, you hear now (whispering behind her hand) cos they'll stretch you out like a clowns pocket, and damage you for life.' to which hastily I nodded, as if my life depended on her sound advice.

And so like this, the hostel revolved around me - the hostel girls truly cared - they were my sisters. Even the cooks had a soft spot for me, and were all over me like kisses on a baby's butt. Recalling Mini: a fat, happy, big-titted Chandee cook, who'd babysit and suckle me and change my nappies. And Sophie: a fat, happy, big-titted Pureto cook, who'd pamper me with her tits and powder my bum. And so you could say my life was safe and sweet, as one can image, when all women want to do is feed you "tit" and play with your with little ding-a-ling all day long.

* * *

And as a scrawny kid with big ears—Johnny Snakes would be served breakfast in bed, always with a pack of cigs on the side; spoilt rotten by his black-crowned Chaykeetin ma'am.

And later when Johnny was ugly enough to take care of himself—he lied about his age, and went off to fight in the War of Broken Wills—enlisting at the bold age of 16.

And as a physical instructor in the service, Johnny Snakes would lay flat on his back, and with a boyish wink signal a fellow soldier, stood over him with a brick, to have that thing smashed down into his chest or abs. And *PIOING!*—that brick would ricochet off Johnny Snakes like a rubber bullet bouncing off a country lane wall. Johnny relishing demonstrations *that* exhibited his physical strength; inspiring the lads, and sending a warning to the enemy that they were about to catch a thousand degrees of comeuppance. This cocky demonstration of crazy vitality, Johnny's way of showing the mental and physical condition the army expected the boys to champion. Johnny Snakes forging the boys into full-fledged warriors: hard as anvils—each of them of the belief they were equal to ten of the enemy.

And Johnny Snakes served with the "Dog Soldiers", 1st Infantry Division or The Dukes as they were known, a brutal and aggressive outfit that fought in all the major battles of the war campaign. Johnny Snakes recalling an ominous sight that he and the boys happened upon: a solitary enemy tank—its crew members still in their assigned positions, faces calm, eyes staring dead ahead - not even as much as a scratch on them. Just a trickle of blood from a nostril or ear. All dead by concussion.

Which in this case must have occured from a high explosion that burst over the turret top—sucking out all the air and sending shock waves through the tank—causing everyone's brain, under the immense pressure, to pop inside their skulls.

And Johnny Snakes taught me: "Body size matters nothing in time of war, son. The only thing that counts is balls. True man-sized balls."—Telling me of these big macho blokes, thinking themselves all tough and invincible. But when the bombs dropped, those self-same guys were caught rattling in their cots (down in the bunkers) crying for their mommas—shitting in their pants through fear and panic.

And when I asked Johnny Snakes what it felt like to take another man's life, he looked at me; secretly tearful, going: "Son, it feels like waking up for the first time. War is no joke, it changes a man. Cos the moment you take a life, that stays with you. You can never forget it. Every sensation, the smell of the air, your heart pounding in your chest, the cold realization that you've just taken a life, that stuff never leaves you. Why I can still feel it now, that moment I took a life for the first time, it's like it was yesterday. (Sighs) But I did what I had to do. And I don't feel any guilt about it either. It is what it is. It's just... the whole act of killing in war, that gets confusing - cos it's not personal, you know, and maybe on a different day the man you killed might have been your friend; someone not so different from you with family or kids, someone with problems and passions, who is also trying to navigate their way through this life, trying to evolve and better themselves, a someone who goes from being this force, this expressive vitality with big hopes and aspirations, to the smallest nothing - you can smack it, beat it, throw rocks at it, but it can do nothing back to you. And you are the one responsible for that, you are the one that took all the life and dreams away from them, and that's what makes war sad."

And Johnny Snakes had many stories about the war. But one in particular made him proud. His eyes burning with a rich and deep warm bronze; glinting, as he revealed the event:

It was a sunny day—September 1945, when Johnny Snakes and his Division: responsible for peacekeeping duties in the overthrown country of Brulé, received orders to pull out the area. Along with instructions to dump all their rations. And so emptying their packs—containing mainly biscuits and tins of 'bully', they pierced the tins with bayonets and threw everything into a huge ditch; covering it over. A terrible waste. However, what made it even worse was that the order had to be carried out in front of a camp of starving prisoners of war. But these were not hardened soldiers - no - they were just ordinary civilians of Brulé - no more than two meters away - men, women, children; babies, packed behind rusted barbed wire—crying, begging them not to bury the food. It was a sickening crush to the spirit. Something that Johnny Snakes didn't want to be apart of - saying that if he didn't man-up and deal with that moment in the right way - his actions would have determined the kind of man he would've ended up being. Cos Johnny, like all legends, knew exactly what honor meant. And he wasn't the only one - the guys in his regiment felt the same. But they'd be court-martialed, stripped rank, and imprisoned if they attempted to give their rations to the starving, who now looked on woefully as the smell of sweet meat caused bellies to rumble and stab with hunger. It was a living curse. A god-awful shame... Especially seeing the helpless ones: babies, chunking their eyes out; nostrils blocked with snot, attracting flies - their dirty little angel faces, streaked with tears, as they stretched out bony, weak arms—pleading through the thorned-wire—grabbing at the image of the buried rations - now nothing more than a fat belly of earth. And some of them already were so weak they dropped like flies. The entire camp echoing a cry that droned like a mindless mass mantra that hung in the palpable summer's glare like that of doom.

And for Johnny Snakes there was no way of making sense of something so irrational. And what he did next, ended up being a heroic move. With his shovel he cut the earth and began to dig up all the rations. And just like that, one kind deed, electricity filled the air like a supernatural surge, and all of a sudden, there was an energetic shift in consciousness that blanketed the region, peoples buzzing, as every man in Johnny's regiment in seeing the light, did the right thing and began to help Johnny, who looking up, saw now a wall of prisoners looking at him and his fellow soldiers—the hope in their eyes priceless. And because of Johnny and the men who disobeyed a direct order, obedient to the voice in their hearts, today, the children who survived that prisoner camp, as a result of a good deed, are now telling their grandkids the same story.

* * *

And granddaddy Snakes always had new stories to impart - things he wanted me never to forget - images for my mind to re-run like survival guides: detailing the shit he had endured as a young man and how he remained strong and resilient throughout it all, keeping that dream always on edge.

And when Johnny Snakes got back from the war—chesting-out his proud pins: big medals displayed—having killed all the enemy he could lock his gun on; for the sake of placing peace in his soul, he went straight to church to balance his karma - struttin' through the church doors in dress uniform traditional to The Dukes - draped down in a kilt—with socks pulled up to his knock-knees. Johnny Snakes waltzing in with Granny Snakes (then known as Mavis Snakes) latched to his arm and feeling that rush of manly pride and youth that goes with fast livings and good vibrations. His big balls swaying like huge wreckin' weights between muscular thighs. Johnny Snakes, indeed, being all he could be—ready to receive redemption. But soon enough, as the excitement settled - Johnny smelt *shit* in the air. His eager *ear-to-ear* toothless-gash turning from juicy joy to tight-lipped disgust. As the whole congregation—or rather, contagion; loyal to the very regime Johnny had fought to overthrow, turned round now—shaking their heads in disapproval of all the flaunted brass, bronze and silver medals that hung off the President's ribbons; pinned to Johnny's dress jacket.

And being away at war so long, Johnny Snakes forgot just how loyal to the old system the people of his old community really were, plus how much he himself had changed. His presence evoking hostility. Each brainwashed supporter of the Old Order still reeling from the hard bring down of the "promised orgasm": a well-designed deception they all got sold short on. As now, with cruel hawk faces, they clustered on Johnny - this plucky young soldier; swaggering into their mournful midst, something to target their hate on. Johnny Snakes' presence a symbolic emblem of the big reason why they'd lost the war. And so now the lynch was on. And poor Johnny, finding his hot-hide not amongst his fellow countrymen, had to kick his gears *once more* into war mode. But even as mad and tough as Johnny Snakes was, he foresaw a showdown here as a losing game. For he knew he couldn't wrestle them all at once. And so giving Ma Snakes a big wet kiss; telling her to escape out the fire exit, he bolted—*PSHOOING!*—gone—sailing over pews like a champion hurdle-hound. His heavy, hairy scrotum cheekily slapping one old geezer on the forehead *SLAP!* leaving a salty wet patch between the old boy's baby blues, every fucker now in that God-house going beserk, throwing their Bibles and chorus books at Johnny's bony cranium—the whole goddamn congregation of burning God-lovers bowling down the church steps chasing after Johnny Snakes.

But quicker than a sailfish on a deadbait-line, Johnny charged a tear-up trajectory, as like a lithe twister with intent—he left them all flat, choking on his dust. Yep, my good ole granddaddy Johnny Snakes - a man who had balls the size of planets.

* * *

Yep. Poor granddaddy Snakes, who eventually bit the bullet when a cancer bug killed him. Ate his lungs up and choked his breath out. And when the doctor pumped him full of radium to kill the cancer bug, he withered away in a hospice for the doomed, dying in his son's arms—having fulfilled his passion's purpose—ready for insertion into some next simulation.

11.

JESSE RAPIER

BETWEEN rosy walls - in a bedroom with burglar-barred windows - *there* on my antique fold-down writing desk, sat my light sea-green Olivetti Lettera 22—along with several bottles of writing ink, a rough draft of my theatrical play High Tea, and Violets in a clay pot.

In one corner stood a shelving unit rammed-tight with all kinds of reads. Sweetly aromatic, vanilla scented reads. Yellow-brown and musky reads. Reads with amber cello taped spines, and those with their library flaps, date stamps and pencil codes still inside. There were damaged, dog-eared reads - musty-looking, tired, tattered and chipped reads - gently aged reads - and reads barely even touched. But amongst all these classic, bold monuments to literature, stood one read in particular—my first pebble into the crab-meat sea (my poor attempt at being a great poet), a 78-page misdemeanor, entitled: Assassins and Aliens, published by Fatback Books—a small publishing company out in the well-to-do suburb of La Cresta Village, Backwood—run by the infamous Jesse Rapier: essayist, poet, landlord and womaniser, who by the time we met, boasted bedding over a hundred women; whores excluded.

Jesse Rapier was about ten years my senior, and in 1994, the man responsible for taking me to my first ever live sex show, at a place called Seventh Heaven, deep in the heart of Backwood, L'Shasta Street.

Jesse Rapier knew the doorman at Seventh Heaven - a thin, gaunt, dangerous looking fella, who let us in for free—when normally you'd have to cough up 50 buckskins—a lotta "coin" in them days - considering how many beers you could buy.

I was excited and appeased to say the least—laden with a firm sack of penance—waking up in the *middles* of the night with a painful hard-on and "blues" that gave me murders so baaad, I coulda chopped my own tool off - if it weren't for the saving graces of sticky pussy meat to unload my gold spasms into. And that's the thing about "youth". You can tug on your piece six times a day—throttling that beast as if trying to iron out the skin folds on a turkey neck - going the whole good mile, frantically jerking out that hot load - clenching that pelvic muscle (with eyes pleading shut) ready to receive hot deliverance—that curdle deep inside BUILDING to a sweet little melt - until finally - having kept it on edge as long as you can - all you can do is bow to the burn and exhale as a static jolt zaps through your body - to which - in opening your eyes, you realize, you've just spunked all over Grammy's mustache.

But now on my way to Seventh Heaven, I had no thoughts of self-pleasure, or adorning Grammy's mantel. For all I wanted was the freedom to douse my blues *in*-some hot trickling pussy. Tough chance here though, given that them whores keep their privates cold as Eskimo guts.

Bundling into a nervous knot, my stomach did flick-flacks and my heart weakened at the knees, as I climbed the stairs to Seventh Heaven.

Straight off I got hit by the air: sweltering with the hot musk of feral pussy. And then - there they were. We, "the meat" had found our predators. Like lionesses at some watering hole, deep in goddess black Māratopia—with stars out like gems in the night, at the bar, there they stood - these sexually magnetic dames of the night - all dusky hued and reminiscent of rock iguanas: cold-blooded, dinosaur-like creatures—dripping in fake diamonds and all dolled-up in mortician's make-up—eyes shimmering with Proloxytin and Xycamorphinol—smoking menthols and sipping diluted spirits, eyeing out each man as a potential player—their skins crawling with a magnetic undulance.

And that's one thing about a whore. She's a rite of passage. A portal to the other world. For by fucking a whore - entrance is gained to the open road. A prerequisite for all true, warrior-artist, savage beastlike men.

* * *

Inside, the place was decked out like a sports café. Television sets mounted on the walls. The volume turned down - showing nothing but hard-core porn, non-stop. Big juicy cocks. Huge, shaven, skin-slapping balls. Semen on fries. Blood smattered shit burgers. Pain given. Pain taken. Degradations and bondage. Creampies and big silicone injected titties. Squirt Queens and piss-garglers. Every kind of slutty defilement beaming like brainwash drip-torture. The raw, the awful and the liberated. Every way-out scene of sex ALL for your entertainment. Images to color your mind, melt your heart, and make you lose your soul, all ready to be lubed up, probed and injected with sleaze.

And being in such a place, all that visual stimuli, plus the girls walking around butt naked - smelling of stewed sex and horse piss, one whiff alone was enough to make you erect— jumping your heart from its socket and breaking you to your knees: begging for that sweet honey like some lowly hound. Yep, this was a den of lustful deeds; a shelter of flesh that was the ultimate amusement park for the sexually-charged fiend. The world out there now ceased to exist. You couldn't help but sense you were in another dimension, once you stepped inside Seventh Heaven.

At the far end of the place stood a stage with a catwalk that lead off - surrounded by groups of sweaty men on bar stools, hollering and hooting in drunken mirth - brazenly breathing out cigar and cigarette smoke like big bloat kings - all of 'em *same time* (like kittens) looking up in tame adoration at the birdy on the branch - bootlickers the lot of 'em, all worshipping them whores up there (on stage) - fearless sirens, stripped to their shaven crotches: spotlit and star burnt, as down amongst us on the butt-crushed, beer-spilt floor, flesh mongers traipsed—balancing on clear stilettos—stirring the air with sweat and pheromones—offering potential customers "rumpy-pumpy" in the backrooms.

Now of all the rooms, the sauna was best, for at only 300 buckskins, you could get an hour with two whores - not to mention the bottle of bubbly thrown in gratis; sweetening the deal. The other rooms such as the sadomasochism, the massage and fantasy room—for 150 buckskins, allowed you only 30-minutes to let off your "bang!" with just one whore.

Once the girl up on stage concluded her striptease, she'd begin fingering herself—sucking each finger glistening wet—inserting one, then two, three, four, until she was up to her wrist in pussy. Her entire fist shoved up her cookie jar - reminiscent of the kid unwilling to loosen their grasp on the object of their desire - trapped via possession. These whores loving the money, the free drugs, the rockstar-like adoration, the rich sugar daddies - things desperate people just can't let go of.

* * *

The swaggering effects of alcohol, and the rowdy fever of having so many bit players slobbering, wheezing, panting (in such a confined space) - plus the garnishing funk of feral pussy, made Seventh Heaven an intoxicating launch pad HOT into the bedrock of the sun. The general feeling here: that everyone in tow, where all members of the same fire-and-dance, sweat-orchestrated, sexually ritualistic underground slave-workshop; worshipping the understandings of our own making. Each one roll-called and cashed-in on the same clock card. A gross honorance of the journeying rapture. Everyone swept away on that ONE BIG Auspicious Trip. Our collective trance—pushing our souls to the next big thunder-awakening; embracing a new dimension. The super-hot atmosphere - along with the cool, fevered-up women, slamming the place with edge. Them rattlesnake whores, each one, like ritualistic oracles, mediums—guiding us to the portal reckoning, as they performed their slow, luring, ballet; entrancing everyone, who by now - super-sensually and telepathically locked-in - all converged in the attainment of that one ultimate communiqué of ascension.

And stepping down now from stage to catwalk, with a vibrating dildo in hand, the whore offered each guy a turn at inserting the vibrator in-and-out of her stray, gluttonous pussy. Her effervescent eyes bright with bully confidence. Each guy knowing [just] what this little sacrament had brought on. For it was time. This meaningful act of passing the sacred baton all part of the evening's climax. The one thing every man had been holding out for. Time for that Vampirella up there, that golden-topped girl with the long hard life and drugs in her eyes, to be worshipped. As now from the doe-eyed crowd—she was ready to choose one lucky guy to join her up on that 'catwalk-altar' for LIVE *flashing* SEX - stripping "you" bare - stroking you - rolling on a condom - sucking your chop - cupping and twisting your nut sack in her long-clawed paw - giving your Dr Willard Johnson a few playful strokes - the odd heat bubble rising in your balls, as throwing her dirty eyes into your skull - plaguing your heart with lust - doing things with her tongue - sending ripples crashing through your brain; making your eyes roll around in your skull as if you'd been *shmacked up* with fever, yep, she'll do all dem tings - making you feel broad-chested and in charge of the world - all invincible and shit like a beast with its game on.

And on that night I just had a sinking feeling. For when she looked at me, I knew I was sacrificial meat. And no sooner had the thought occurred, when with curled finger, she beckoned me. The crowd parting like a mythical sea. And then, as if under a spell, I began gravitating toward her. Stepping up onto that catwalk altar—I stood vulnerable in front of that Goddess of the Night: a crafty, raw, love machine, with cigarette burns and bruises on her body. A strange, intriguing woman, sad and callose-kneed from endless doggie style sessions on bitter brown rugs in ratty dives, she being the original Motel Queen. And so after the introductory foreplay - she laid herself down, spreading her glory—revealing that magenta ruby - acting out her part by design as the Desperate Enchantress of Illusion, Death and Rebirth, as she flashed me a reassuring smile.

I felt my ass cheeks blush and my asshole pucker up, as knelt in front of her, bowing to the crowd, I accepted my fate: just another chunk of meat in the meat parade, ready for the butcher's slab. The whole place (by this point) on the verge of eruption. The men raising the roof—chanting, building the tension, as grabbing my balls by the neck, pausing, she gave me a longing look. And then VOILA!—she fed me inside her cold scraps. Touchdown! Fuck me! I was plugged in! A full-throated cheer exploding, as in that victorious moment the whole place erupted like "home winnings" on Saturday night.

Suddenly, an ecstatic shudder grabbed me like a death grip. Her pussy nodes latching on and sinking hooks into every nerve in my body; siphoning off all my energy. But I was up for the tussle - fighting the Kryptonic powers of her wonder pussy, as shrugging off them initial effects, licking my finger, I slicked down my eyebrow and I went at it - *WHAM! BAM!* full torque, straight to work like a cool pussy-mechanic, as I pounded out the kinks in her bone-chilling pussy. Her skin smooth as whipped cream served with dark cherries, as knees up with dainty toes curled, she dug red marks with jockey heels into my buttocks; pushing me deeper inside her ceremonial love jar. Gawd! My finger lickin' soul ready for blast-off *at this point*, as leaping from my body I shot up like a pyrotechnic star deep into blissful space.

Gawd! This was thee most intense *sexperience* ever. For being plugged into that whore, I experienced something akin to an outer body projection, as now down below, I witnessed my body doing acts I no longer was a part of. For it was an epic performance now. No longer was I there for myself. I was now the admired—the cajoled—the Bronco savant—the Elvis matador in his suit of lights *down on bended knee*—rattling fingers *blinged-out* in gold signets: index finger pointing *legend* to the stars, as jigging away—punishing the lip-licking malice of this strange, wonderful, unforgettable, hard-hitting dame with her power to disturb the hearts of men, I bounced her up stratospherically and glided her gently back down—making her feel all true, and real, and woman-like again. Her heart gushing deliriousness, as filled with a wanton lust for that ALL unconscious-consuming thrill—blown to the stars in the throes of orgasm, she shook—sucking hisses—loving every inch of my cock that caressed her thirsty walls. My blood-engorged manhood dinging her hot button until all too much—shivering and shaking like a voodoo witch in a white-eyed trance - she - that hardheaded woman, broke in my arms to become the softest most beautiful substance known to man: a pleasured woman.

12.

REBELLION, DEATH, AND BLACK MAGIC

Peering into the candle at my bedside, I took a deep breath, grabbed the matchbox from my granddaddy's coat; unwrapped each tiny gold bead (from their aluminium foil packaging)—and with a wry smile that said: "See ya later, son"—I popped them three "Starfalls" under my tongue.

25 minutes into "It" and I started to "come up" already—a fluttering anxiety churning deep within my gut; the telltale factor I was well on my way, as objects NOW began to appear brighter, vibrant—some even breathing.

Quickly I darted into the kitchen and poured myself a glass of water. On my way back, I noticed the lounge light was still on but the TV off - a sign my mother was working on the last of her crosswords, before heading off to bed.

I returned to my room, sat on the edge of my bed and waited for the portal reckoning. Suddenly a breeze brushed my cheek and the hair back-of-my-neck stood up. IT WAS THE PARADIGM SHIFT. This was it. And already I could feel the pull 'n' plumber - a gut thrust, as 1-2-3-GO!!! I got sucked into the void.

Immediatly I sensed a universal connection with everything—as gazing upon this new realm like an open-mouthed, beam-faced convert - everything now appeared ALIVE and VIVID - emblazoned with a bubbling crayon-like color. Each dripping splash of creative sensitivity pouring into me like sweet molten molasses. Each alchemic thrust and masterful stroke hard-bitten and purposeful, overpowering my soul, as in-and-out, in-and-out; rooted deep, punching the cervix and breaching the womb of awakening—I received downloads from the astral plane. The cosmic plunder of intel penetrating my subconscious *with* a pure and undefiled ecstasy that made me writhe like a giddy virgin ravaged by a glory of unicorns. Every super-erotic sperm-driblet of fizzing nectar forming pulchritudinous works of art that resembled blazing planets set against the jet of night - surrounded by combustions of reigning princely glitters and explosions of color that blitzed the eyesight, searing fiery images into my retinas, as HELD suspended in temporary blindness, gradually, in patterns of crazy scattered light, forms faded back into focus—everything buzzing anew and cupped within this fantastic floating shamanistic realm of wonder that oozed transcendental evanescence.

I rose to my feet and was met sidelong with an oscillation in frequency - my mind roused and roving, when head-on, HIT by another wave of thrashing anxiety, a spellbinding energy split right through me (my eyes *a-shimmer*) as an intense sensation came upon me like that of lukwarm bucket loads of water being poured down my back.

The corners of my mouth began to curl into ludicrous barbed hooks - arousing my face with a stupid grin that would not let go. I then started to giggle, unable to stop, followed by moments of subsidence and relief with me going, 'Pheeew!'—as again, that rising sensation of lukewarm water rushed down my back. It was beautiful and maddening all that the same time. An eccentric unsteadiness that went from one spike of hilarity to the next.

I then collapsed onto my bed into insane fits of chuckles and hurls that make it hard to breathe. My cheeks aching from the permanent smile plastered upon my face.

The effect of those three "Starfalls" were monstrous; and I still had the peak to look forward to. Suddenly, I began to feel elsewhere, funny, freakish; crazy-on-edge - just another hardstone rebel with a shotgun soul running a secret errand of no return.

REBELLION, DEATH, AND BLACK MAGIC

And then I did something really bad, I cursed my trip …

I brought a barbed-wing darkness down upon my head. My "trip" tusked with epic horns, as throwing the "mad switch", I flooded my room with a five hundred carat stone-cold surge of pure low vibrational presence.

In a fool's attempt to straighten the immoderate giggles and my erratic hysteria, I commanded out loud: 'No! Be serious!'—and upon these three grim words, with my intention calibrated, the universe responded. An EMP of *my heart's desire POOMING!* a reaction that set off a zero gradient ping on the vector grid; kicking-off a crunch down factor likened to a gaunlet-throwdown, as stood toe-to-toe with the deep unknown, I caused my entire "trip" to implode. I was now going-gone-SOLID; beyond damage control. My "utterance", like a spell detonator had triggered the fine print buried deep within the architecture of the drug, activating a still open astral realm contract agreed upon eons ago, as all the other timelines and alternate dimensions now buzzed and felt the shift. It was nothing short of a rude awakening of the dormant chromosome that all along lay in wait for this bubbling hot moment.

Everything altered. A high-powered dark presence swept over my room. The temperature dropped, and the air hung malodorously like a plague, as then suddenly; snatched away, I was no longer in my room—stood now thigh deep in a field of wheat all bathed in neon blue and dwarfed by gargantuan pylons towering like huge clotheslines draped with electrocuted human flesh; hung out like trophies of some eternal hunting game. Was this a snapshot of the Trophy Room of Life. Was this place where all things are decided, vile and grisly as any torture chamber.

* * *

Then, like cannons—*BOOM! BOOM! BOOM!*—a bright blinding light accompanied by the rumbling of thunder blew above me

- and there it was—an orange circular symbol HUGE, the size of a vast coliseum—looming and glowing and pulsating and turning above me. It's power resembling a gigantic bug zapper that drew-me-in with its magnetic intricacy as it blazed ALIVE like some hot branding iron pulled straight from the heart of the sun—ready to "freedom-brand" my wild rawhide-soul.

And within the orange symbol, were three smaller circles. And between the circles were symbols and lettering. The outer set of symbols and lettering turned counter-clockwise. The middle set, clock-wise. And the inner set as the outer—as now unnervingly—the atmosphere revved with a mad, psycho, pipe-organ motorcade of grinding gears and whizzing sparks. Somehow, I had entered the pit of the machine as throttles twisted red-faced—causing my brains to smoulder and burn like sacrificial meat on throbbing embers.

Then, in an instant *THOOM!* I was back in my room again. The orange symbol was there too, as if having followed me from the otherside - watchful - the symbol now though a lot smaller: the circumference of hula hoop—as pulsating with a fiery deep trembling thud—it held me transfixed like someone with savant syndrome blasting me out - making me feel absolutely jungle wild and Paleolithic. It was like nothing I'd ever seen—like some magical mark—the mark of awakening I guess—possessing qualities almost mandala-like and zodiacal. The individual smaller symbols I can only describe as being similar to hieroglyphs - timeless and dimentional. In fact the whole sensation of the "trip" felt otherworldly, as if there in my dingy candle-lit room, with a head full of 'Amarantium', I had somehow summoned a force (an Egregore) clearly powerful. A thoughtform indicatively sovereign. Something that spat into the headlights of convention.

* * *

As my "trip" deepened, my room grew colder, and my bedroom walls began to shrink wrap around me. The necrotic reek of ego death intensifying—along with the smothering stench of sulfuric fumes and carrion that hung over my bedroom like a bitter decree.

At the same time now, I couldn't recall anything. I had no past. Didn't know who I was. I felt like nobody in fact. My senses, disconnected. I tried focusing on something, anything, in the hope of retrieving some form of cohesive thought. I set my concentration on the bedside candle, but there AGAIN, inside the flame, like a bad penny, that ancient symbol appeared, only now significantly different—shining with a pure white luminescence—a breathtaking glister, like tinsel from the hottest star.

I stood up and moved about in an attempt to escape the symbol. I looked out my bedroom window, but there to my horror were ghostly faces made-up of smoke, menacingly pressing themselves to the glass. Entities with tortured expressions that frowned a kind of skeletal anguish. Their eye sockets as deep as endless wells, their jaws calcified; locked agape, as if trying to release one endless scream, incapable though of expressing *something* not even they could describe.

I put my nose to the cold glass for a closer, better look, in order to discount this mad hallucination. But as clear as the day I saw death for the first time—there they were. The true face of lost souls screaming in the dark.

13.

MASHED INTO THE SUN-BEATEN GROUND

I was age-5 when I saw someone get killed. A woman crossing the road got run over by a heavy-duty semi. It just plowed right through her; splitting the skin from her legs. The white sinew and bone as blinding as pure sunlit snow.

It took place on one of those hazy hot summer days. The blunt car hooters sounding high over the dry heat and off into the miraging distance, as she, into the sun-beaten ground like fish guts got mashed—wailing a big: 'Why?' whilst dying. Her question going beyond the murk of this matrix to find its way deep into the collective-cloud of past identities. For this Life ain't nothing but a magical and precious dance *with death as the door* into windows of opportunity *to evolve* - passing through this tragic chunk of sensation, thought and emotion, in a hope of taming and molding LIFE into the ideal expression of love.

And when the back wheels of that behemoth truck ran over her trunk, that was it. Dead. Her body squirming and convulsing—flopping about like some mad doomed fish with speechless gills - her dark, frothy blood rolling over the tarmac—mixing with the steaming reek of pungent urine that gushed from her popped bladder. Her nervous system firing out desperate survival messages to twitching limbs; a fight to the end, as uttering choking sounds she gurgled her last words; eyes rolling back into her head. Game Over.

And so, in this moment of true reflextion, tragedy hung over her mangled body like a fresh ritual of endless possibility. A poor, destitute woman, whose DEATH was now seen as just another violent occurrence on an already violent landscape. She, just a little nobody, knocked down in the middle of traffic on one of the hottest days of the year. Her body *still ripe* as the consciousness; vaguely attached, hovered in abeyance. The bloody climax of her life, now nothing more than a bizarre drive-by show, for those peering from their vehicles like parasitic creatures cradled in cozy catatonia: the HOMO SAPIEN; a freak for sure, an educated mistake: unequipped, bare-assed and weak. A hybridized beast, concoted in some pisspot laboratory, aboard a spaceship flown by terraforming hyperdimensional beings, who go around pissing into test tubes *in order to* cook up wretched DNA cocktails *only to* serve up *in our case* a simple-minded, wackadoodle species—who now, getting their daily dose of carnage, stared at that poor woman in the process of crossing over. Her skin, aglisten with sweat, all puffed-up and tough—reeking sweet of rot wine and uncleanliness. Her hard, beautiful face ruined from all them lost years spent quarrelsome sat on curbstones—eyes, cheekbones and mouth smacked swollen. A poor helpless bitch beaten and stomped-on black and blue by men just as mean and ill-fated as her.

And so, unable to pull myself from the scene of her death, counted now among the many that stared; having witnessed every moment of her last dying breath from my school bus window (deep in the journey of being whisked off to school), the eye of my mind refused to let her go: a draining nausea looping through me, turning my world gray, as I wished for nothing else but to lie beside her and stroke her brow. And like this, from the pit of my stomach, to the hot chill in my heart, her death would not leave my skull. Her stretched, pained-face (like that of a mother who had just lost her only child) haunted me.

14.

DAISY LITTLELEAF

THERE was a scratch at my bedroom door—I recognized the knock immediately and opened up, greeted by a short, cute 'Prrrt'. It was Fishy, my cat.

Fishy stuck to me like glue, and was an ever vibrating presence (beside me at all times) whether writing in my room or smoking weed (reclined on a deckchair) or just generally chilling out; baking ballz on the hot-burnt-bricks.

Fishy was runt of the litter, a gray furball of love that grew into an adorable longhaired beauty, full of purrs and dove-like cooings, who became my pet companion and furry cherub—during them long years of unemployment; living with my folks: a neurosis of the times: just another child-god, unequipped to position themself on the path toward success-and-independence. This pinnacle ultimately crowning them with manhood—and that sought after "Alpha" male status.

Now being put up at home, unemployed, presented many temptations. Such as the time I opened up the front door to a gorgeous Chandee woman from the green lands, stood on my front porch, a six string on her back, dressed in a poncho, jeans, cowboy boots and wearing a colorful headscarf. I was familiar with her—she was Daisy Littleleaf, who sometimes would go around neighborhoods doing her own religious cult-like shit; knocking on doors, just to get some random folk to listen to her demo tracks. And often I'd pass her on the street busking for cash, and would flash her a friendly smile or drop in the tin whatever loose change I had - Daisy Littleleaf living miles out in the wildflower paradise of Fawn Meadow.

'Hey there... oh so this is where you stay.' went Daisy. And I was taken aback, thinking: damn, is this chick stalking me or something, as all I could do was flash a smile of surprise. Couldn't believe what was actually happening, though. Daisy Littleleaf? On my doorstep? Get outta here.

'What's the matter, handsome, you secretly in love with me or sumthin'?' Daisy Littleleaf totally out there, literally taking me off-guard. Besides, I didn't know what the fuck else to say. Of course I dug her. She was as cute as fuck. Everytime I'd see her my stomach would do a backflip, making me all weak to the bone and shit. Just like now - totally blown away by this firecracker. But as the first thing came to mind, I just went with it, going: 'Hmm, is that your music?' A pile of CDs in her hand with her face on the cover; what the hell was I thinking.

'You wanna have a listen, genius?'
'Uh? Okay, yeah, we can do it in my room?' My poor choice of words making Daisy giggle out loud. 'Uh, sorry I meant listen to your songs... like, you know...'
Daisy looking at me longingly, going: 'Yeah whatever, like I can't see you want to eat my panties, wild boy?' Daisy pegging me straight away.
With me replying under my breath: 'Hmm, marzipan...'

And letting her in, Daisy graced my home. Her big pious cautious eyes of someone that had stepped both on hallowed ground and into the lion's den itself, as leading her to my room via the kitchen, she followed me closely. And from the moment I opened the door and saw her there; to now, stood in front of me GODDAMN! I buzzed on so many levels of elevated ecstasy that already I was gone in the clouds, maaan. And I'm sure she felt the same. Some primeval wild connection having us both locked into a ritualistic snake dance that hurled us forward with curious excitement and thrilling uncertainty.

Daisy Littleleaf, what can I say, she was totally raw and magnetic. Her tough wood-fire and female body stink *interrupted* by hints of Dragon's Blood fragrance that caused my balls to rumble and my dick to twitch.

I put the kettle on, led her to my room and offered her a seat on my bed, as across from her, at my writing desk—I went: 'Oh, by the way, I'm Freddy.'—and she was like: 'Guess you already know my name, but because you're such a gentleman, Hi, I'm Daisy.' putting out her hand, which I shook, replying: 'Lovely to meet you.' Daisy blushing, as right then and there the energy between us elevated. Our lust radiating as we gravitated from being uncomfortable strangers to sexual soul mates. Though nothing philosophically deep, for I knew I had to keep it straight up simple. And so in order to allow everything to run smooth—with no complicated messages from the heart, it was necessary for me to see Daisy as nothing more than life support for a pussy, which might sound cold and all, but at times you gotta leave emotion at the door, because the plan was for nothing more than cool early afternoon sex, aka a little bit of easy fun.

The kettle clicked, I jumped up, and in my periphery, I caught Daisy easing into her role now. My absence allowing her to relax and browse my room, sat there on my bed, warmed by light from the overspilling sun that poured into my bedroom window.

I served Daisy tea and rusks, put her CD on and sat next to her. I looked at her and saw all her beauty unfold. She, smiling a smile of gratitude, and sipping her tea, while outside in trees swishing, birds swirled in the sparkling sun. It was a good day to be alive in Māratopia, a day of treasure and sexual endeavors and racing thoughts, as my dirty mind now caused my innards to wheel and rumble with a gut burning weakness for that pussy cat between Daisy's sweet thighs.

My folks were not due home for another five hours.

Therefore; I had complete RUN of the house, plus plenty of time to ventilate the place of any "soon to be" heated odors radiating from my bedroom like *hot mud summer lovin's.*

I could barely swallow now, dumb with dizziness. My cock straining against my jeans, as finally, Daisy relaxed, leaning into me while giggling into her palms. For without realizing, I had just given her a funny look similar to that of a mad dog with a rubber band *tightened* around its balls. It was good to see her laugh, knowing she too felt the urge to scratch an itch, as she flashed me a quick look of allurement.

Daisy bit down self-consciously on a rusk, and caught the crumbs, she was absolutely gorgeous. And as she began opening up, I hung onto her every word. I was starting to feel that deep connection I avoided in the beginning, as looking deep inside Daisy's eyes, there was nothing more I or she could say. It was time.

I brushed my fingertips across the nape of Daisy's sticky neck and she whinnied, delirious.

Planting a moist kiss onto her sensitive collarbone, I scooped up her breast and squeezed it. My forward actions causing Daisy to wriggle like a ferret inside a cotton sack. She was loving all the attention, and I guess playing her own little game too. We then began to undress one another, slowly. A sudden sweetness washing over Daisy as I began tracing my fingertips over her soft skin—shooting chills up her spine. I breathed on her skin, kissing her body and sucking her big erect nipples. Her wide black eyes cooing for more, as she lay there beautiful and naked on my bed like a prize.

And so now the moment of truth had arrived, as like a pie-hungry man, I stared endearingly at Daisy's fat pussy-meal as if it were a pouch filled with meaty goodness. I went down on her and started by kissing her inner thighs and all around her pussy.

I avoided the really sensitive areas—allowing her to CRAVE for more. She then opened her juicy legs really wide. I lowered my face right up to her voluptuous blossom, the scent of her sweet musk hitting me like gasoline hitting a raging fire.

'Do you have a condom?' Daisy now wet and ready.

My dick was standing to attention like a proud soldier with his little helmet on, as I searched my desk drawer for my one and only condom—hidden amongst cannabis seeds, empty ink cartridges, crude intoxicated poems, and a stained, unsent luv letter addressed to a short, long-haired, pale Jahrez girl named Katherine—as shooting from my present reality—I got teleported back in time:

Katherine was a girl I stomached love butterflies for, accentuated each time, when in English Lit class, that Kate Bush song: 'Wuthering Heights' got played as "soundtrack" to our set-work book. Cos in my world, Kat and I were the "love-tragic" figures of Emily Brontë's hellish vision of love. For in my misty bohemian gloom—with purple smoke curling from fiery gills and eyes ablaze like giant meteors, I was Heathcliff, and Kat was Catherine my far-off ghostly lover that in gothic dreams I embraced and kissed. For like Heathcliff, I too held sleepless pains for my Kat—sharp-winged butterflies that sliced my heart up, all for the ache of childish love.

Then two seasons later, with a bunch of co-slacker classmates, Kat and I bunked college—tagging a ride in (legend stoner) Craig Bennett's '87 Plymouth Voyager: a roving waste dump for empty beer cans and soda pop bottles, homemade bongs, sweet wrappers, matches, empty rolling paper booklets and chip packets. Every conceivable little gap and groove grouted with weed sweepings, stalks and cannabis seeds. The perfect slow boat on OUR JOURNEY to Smokey Falls to smoke golden weed and blow big billowy clouds of: "Holy shit I'm high!"; smelling Ma Nature. And on that beastly day it was dear slutty Kat who took a steaming dump behind some boulders, and it was HER "nature" we all could smell. The reek of her shit hitting us downwind—bumming our vibe—forcing us to pick-up-sticks to another spot. And as it transpired, it was the same dear Kat, who on that same beastly day, choked on my unwashed pearly knob, laid out cool on a mossy rock, beside crisp clear waters that streamed fresh through fern and undergrowth. And busy like a meat hungry man, I stuck my tongue inside Kat's fat fish-hole—spitting out some old toilet paper (still there from her pre-breakfast piss)—continuing to feed on her flabby guava—smelling the business end of her ass; still ripe from her jobby behind the boulders, as with heads buried in each other's crotches, our easy 69er turned into a hot and hungry little sesh. The lid on Kat's furry pot rattling; boiling juice, as all of a sudden, going into a "sweat shock"—catching spasms, Kat lost it, resembling a run-over cat, as she danced in a dying fit—rolling away in celebration of her orgasm - flying off the mossy rock and landing flat on her back into a trickling rill. Her dirty panties still around her knees, as like king of the castle, I pulled back my skin and spurted my balls into the air 'Urrgh!' my diamond gravy dangling like hot elastic snot off a nearby fern.

* * *

'Let's fucking go!' At last, after rummaging through the past, I found that lonely condom, two years overdue, but rolled it on *anyways;* eager to align for maximum pumpage. Daisy, meantime, laying there, mindless (floating up in a dream)—counting the freckles on my face and falling into my eyes (as I moved onto her) WHEN without even so much as a warning, changing the entry plan, I slipped it in bandit style. And like daybreak, her face beamed one big gap-toothed smile of awe—eyes blinkerty-blink *crystal clear,* as my 8-incher introduced itself to her sweet, musky shit-booth. A predicted full 12 rounds (heavy weight division) on the menu, as I fucked Daisy's brains out like a man serving up hot fig stew. And she was all onboard, chugging with me, going: 'Ohgg! Ohgg! Ohgg! Ohgg!' all open-mouthed and wide-eyed, as ripping right through her shit button; tearing an exit hole three sizes too big, I glimpsed the home straight: that shimmering Love Stone Pire on the horizon, my target ashram, as thirsting the driblets of rising orgasm *wriggling* within her blood (in true lurve warrior style) I kept my bell-dinger *bang* on the mint—hitting all them sweet nodes in her rectum *just right* - making her 'Hock!' several times - *pain and ecstasy* intertwined—her voice, roaring to the rafters (music to my ears) giving me the fuel needed to pound her ass out, as she squealed:

'Ohh! Freddy, Oh, fuck! It's sooo good ... oh, yeah, right there, fuck me ... ohhh, Freddy, yeah, yeah ... ohhhh!' Daisy Littleleaf, a little beast in the sheets - a goddess extraordinaire, taming my wild horses into disrepair.

15.

HIGH AS A SCREAMING DIAMOND

Closing my bedroom door I jumped under the covers, followed by Fishy, who sprang like a locust and curled up against me, when all of a sudden, hearing movement, we both looked towards the window. Fishy swallowed hard, her big beautiful eyes engulfing both our hearts, as in a flash, a tangible presence fell over the room. The curtains moved. But there was no breeze. The windows being shut. Then Fishy stopped purring. Her movements wary. Eyes frightful—as with bobbing head, she turned round at an almost owl-like 270 degrees—half looking at me, fully sensing the palpable unease.

The drug was reigning in now, ruling my senses, as inhaling deep, I sucked in that rich love for life. A thick buzzing suspense filling my lungs and washing over my chest, crashing up my spine and over my skull, as the drug, a seduction, running its fingers through my brain, continued through me, rippling down my neck, rolling off my shoulders and shooting down my arms in sparks that rushed through my body with a blissful radiance that hovered beautifully in my groin; gradually dispersing to my lower limbs. My heart ached as if wanting to stop, but it didn't - it just remained beating, shaking me to the core—sending a steady Morse code of light that gave a warm wink to the Ferryman *in wait* at the heart of the abyss. As now, high as a screaming diamond, with an insane waterfall of passion cascading through me, my eyes rolled back into their hallucinogenic sockets, and I quivered in ecstasy.

The drug was immense—and showed no sign of slackening as it steam-plowed a mean course through my being, as the only thing left to do was relinquish all knowledge of self. But then something unexpected happened. Another dramatic dark shift in consciousness. Something sinister. As falling into a trance, I began uttering these long, crazed ramblings; curses, that were like cantations in a language of a cryptic vernacular. And then, taking a match and igniting it, I lowered it to my arm, and watched (void of emotion) as the red-hot tip seared into my flesh—creating a bubbling little hole in my arm, where the fat and flesh cooked. And this went on for a while. The same cryptic words continuing to fall from my lips, like some malign, coded-affirmation, as again, I repeated my tiny ceremony of self-harm.

* * *

And after hours of insanity, finally the drug had run its course. The orange symbol had disappeared for good now; though deep-seated, it remained etched into my consciousness like some benchmark scar.

Outside, life gradually began to QUAKE. The day cutting through the veil of twilight, as chittering amongst themselves with chests heaved out proud, starlings burst (big and triumphant) into morning song. Their iridescent little coats catching the light in sparkles of deep greens, exploding purples, and mottles of brilliant gold that whizzed and fired in electric flecks, as with hearts puffed and heads raised—opening their beaks, they rolled PRAISES for the new day. Their little heads crowned by glorious rays from the dynamite sun.

* * *

Paranoia, a result of vitamin deficiency, plus constipation, and rising toxicity, bad peception, old belief, and ill confidence, all crept into my heart, making me feel as though I'd been singled out in a line-up of oldtime villains, rebels and wastrels, guilty of some buried crime deep beneath the layers my own karma, as now from the house, various sounds began to stir. And unable to distinguish what they were, the worst of thoughts attacked. My head still fizzling, whining aloud with mechanized blood that lead me to imagine strangers were in the house; moving objects or furniture about OR worse, that a break-in was taking place, as holding myself still, with hardly a breath; afraid to make a peep—I feared that if they heard as much as the rise and fall of my chest, they'd kick the door down and slaughter me in bed. But when I heard a familiar sound, it struck me, shit, it was only my dad moving about, getting ready for work. 'Pheew.' It was only Ricky Snakes.

16.

RICKY SNAKES

RICKY Snakes stood in the mirror and tattooed the name "Bonny" (some unforgettable fuck) on his upper right arm. A sewing needle dipped in India Ink piercing his skin, as dark lines streamed down—collecting at his fingertips—dripping into a pool of blood and ink at his feet.

He was out of it, young, stoned, muscular and street tough. These being the wild buck days when Ricky Snakes hung teachers out of classroom windows, and got stuck into Kingswood vs. Deadboro gang brawls. Them good ole days when gangs went-at-it with fists, bats and chains. But it wasn't only in gangs that Ricky Snakes fought: the night three dudes tried jumping him and my mom, who, romantically, Ricky Snakes met age-19—working as a bouncer. And at the door, he checked her ticket, and looked into her eyes, and from then on it was pure love all the way.

And so anyhow, these three dumbasses ended up cornering Ricky Snakes and my mom (who in them days was still known as Zoë Greenweed) late one night in the legendary streets of Kettle Rock District, Backwood.

Now the first dummy, who tried pulling a move: regretfully laying his hand on my mom—Ricky Snakes grabbed his fingers and snapped them off like twigs. And then in no time, while dummy number one was screaming in agony—Ricky Snakes pounced on dummy number-two. All he had to do was edge forward and *Ka-dush!* - a headbutt straight to the face. And as a mature man in his 60s, Ricky Snakes recounted: 'I got him a classic shot, son, you shoulda seen it; a real beaut—the guy's nose opened up like a flower.' And then it was onto dummy number-three—who was real easy—for with his boxing know-hows gained from punch-up rounds down in the sweaty school gym; knowing just where to plant the winner came as second nature—as Wham-o!—Ricky Snakes landed a clean shot straight to the guy's jawbone—Bam!—right on the button. The guy flumping to the floor like a sack of cooked turds. And that was it—"overs ka-dovers" (in record time). And when my daddy's mate, cousin and uncle came out of the club and saw what these dummies were up to—they put the boot in, and taught those hoodlums an old school lesson. Their heads kicked in against the curbstone—teeth rolling out their heads like unlucky dice - as streams of blood flowed into a storm drain.

And after that night, word around town warned: 'No one FUCKs with Ricky Snakes.'—Who in them days stood proud like a shining, young Robert Redford—hand slouched in pocket—leaned up on his muscular shoulder against the local corner shop—dressed in a white tee, white jeans and desert boots—hitting swigs off a pint of milk and radiating *that* "don't-fuck-with-me" cool. Ricky Snakes, who in these youngblood days—with a band of fellow Kingswood boys, got marshaled out of town by the law for scouring the streets, breaking windows on their way—ending their avalanche of mayhem in the docks - brawling—beating up a bunch of sailors WHO anchored with virgin sea-lungs and brains fresh with Cheyneecian arrogance that got hammered out by tough, street-fighting fists—backed-up by "to-the-death" brawn-injected balls...

And so it was right there - stood in the blessed sun; on that corner—beside piled up wooden soda pop crates—that Ricky Snakes day-dreamed rolling down the road in a bright red fire engine with sirens yelling *Bee-aa-baa-chi!* The thrill-bone rush of it! Storming into blazing buildings, blood pumping—balls flying—side by side with fellows of the Fire Brigade—fighting to douse the writhing flames of that RED HOT monster—squared-

RICKY SNAKES

up toe-to-toe like mighty men from those days gallant in blood baths on fields of battle.

And I'd love visiting the Fire House. The smell of the polished jasper floors and waxed wooden tiles. The freshly brassoed doorknobs, skirting and switch plates—everything immaculate and shipshape all round. The men out each day in the courtyard—doing drill practice. And come lunch time or supper time; anytime, all meals were prepared by the men (in rotation) - after all, it was home-away-from-home—everyone taking pride in their Fire House.

And when Ricky Snakes brought home his fireman helmet and axe—I'd wear them—running through the house—pretending to be a fire engine. His helmet still sweet with the rich scent of leather and sweat—mixed-in with the toasty smell of smoke—usually right after a fresh firefight.

And Ricky Snakes, who I'm proud to call my daddy, would pass on some gems, telling me: "Sometimes the biggest lesson a man's gotta learn is to mother himself, son. To suck back the tears and choke on the milk of life that is pain. The pain of mistakes the ultimate weaning factor that grows a boy into a man made by tough choices. A man moulded and cut out of granite by the hammer and chisel of experience."

And in them days Ricky Snakes ate mountains for breakfast—running up and down Mount El Morro each day, on only a stomach of toast, beaten eggs and coffee—just to raise his heart and clear his mind; ready for duty. And in his days as a fireman - Ricky Snakes saw it all. Things that would've molded any man into a seasoned leather punch bag of tough bones and hardened nerves—seeing what he did in his 20-years of service—confronting death daily - such as a decomposed body beneath a carpet of bubbling maggots—mostly the aged—no family or loved ones to pop round to check up on them. And in such cases the men had to bust the door down; wearing their BA's (Breathing Apparatus), the stench so bad it would make your boots curl. Then suicides—often someone who'd just blown their brains out. And as a fireman you have to go into people's homes - the parents or loved ones breaking down (hysterical), while you're there on all fours - picking up goops of blood, brain and skull. And then road accidents—bodies struck at high speed—limbs detached on impact - torn from their sockets. And your job as a fireman is to search for any missing body parts. But the most thrilling part of being a fireman is fighting the monster itself - forests on fire, squatter camps, house fires, giant blazes, flames rippling through buildings—factory fires - Ricky Snakes recalling a massive blaze they fought at an ink factory - tackling the beast, drenched in sweat and water - pores packed with soot. Ricky Snakes and the men, after they defeated the beast, their tunics, helmets, boots, and faces all covered in fantastic color. And also there'd be magnificent scenes of nature going up—walls of fire raging on the Dallameer Mountain Range that burned for days - fanned ablaze by strong winds—a spectacular inferno by night—beautifully reflected against a black sky infused with the orange rich tones of Ma Nature's fury. And there'd also be the grim fires that claimed human lives. MANY in one go—entire informal settlements razed *flat-pack* to the ground. The only sign people once inhabited the area were the skulls and bones smouldering scattered like some unceremonious primitive sacrificial offering. And even gang shootings they'd attend—patching up the wounded or holding hands with the dying, all apart of the job. Plus drownings, all kinds of DEATH—cradling a lifeless infant in ones arms. Onto ship fires, chemical spills, you name it—Ricky Snakes had seen it all in his twenty years as a fireman.

And looking at me with tough, hooded greens with gold flecks—Ricky Snakes told me of a call-out attended, one rainy night:
    A motor had plowed straight into the back of a truck—and

landed up beneath it. The driver decapitated with his intestines twisted around the driveshaft. And so Ricky Snakes and the men had to unravel that dead guy's guts, looking as it did like fried meat on a red-hot rotisserie. The guy's head was found on the backseat, a distorted scream stretched across his horrified face.

And again, yet another crash. This time early bells, Ricky Snakes and the men receiving the call at two in the morning. And ready for action: out of bed and into their boots they sprang ALERT!—especially Ricky Snakes, who back then drove the fire pump—IT being a ruling: "Responding to a call you must be out the station within a minute, and not a second longer." As all aboard—the men held fast while Ricky Snakes worked that big-boned machine—going around bends and hugging tight lines—chucking that plow-run down-slope—"Determined to reach that call for help", threading that tank-assed bitch into the eye-of-the-needle—through narrow neighborhoods and congested traffic—captaining that big wheeled bladder masterfully through the roads, streets and trails of Māratopia *blindfolded.*

And arriving at the scene - they found the remains of a '69 Mustang Boss 429 strewn across the road—the engine block lying several meters away—the vehicle cut in half—the speedometer clocking 128 mph. An assessment of the scene determining that the driver misjudged the bend, hit the pedestrian island and rolled a few times. Ricky Snakes and the men checked everywhere for "victims", as the call-out specifically said, "persons trapped". Eventually they found the "victim". The driver, who turned out to be the only person involved, was discovered stone dead in the boot. The impact of the crash so tremendous - the guy literally looked like a sardine in a tin can the way he was wrapped in wreckage.

Regular occurrences of shack fires also exposed the horrific side of the job—especially when entire communities got snuffed out. For the thing with "shack fires" is, being so close-knit, if one shack goes up—all the surrounding shacks go up with it. And in the slums, because the majority of people use LPG (Liquid Petroleum Gas) cylinders to cook food and boil water with, there is always the risk of fire - especially when a portable braziers containing hot coals used to heat up the drafty shacks with, is left to smoulder day and night. And because of the limited space - the average shack no larger than a double bedroom - and people being people - lazy or forgetful or just too damn drunk, out of ignorance, an LPG cylinder sometimes gets left too close to the red-hot brazier. And if you know how heat properties work: when the flash point of the material in question is reached you get a response alright.

And when the liquid in an LPG cylinder reaches its boiling point - *KA-BOOM!* it is literally a bomb. And if you're not killed by the shrapnel that can take your head off or hit a main artery— in an enclosed area it will most certainly burst your eardrums.

And after such an incident—Ricky Snakes recalled how early one morn in Strawbell Township—after fighting a beast that had turned an entire community to toast—he had to conduct a Search and Retrieval amongst smoky wet piles of corrugated iron: ticking; cooling down. Steaming stacks that were once peoples homes now resembling a battlefront aftermath. For as far as the eye could see, ruins hissed. The white Māratopian sands dirtied a copper-brown by the sun filtering through a hunchbacked billow of doom that hung casting its shadow over Strawbell Power Station, while scattering ash upon Nazteko Cemetery. The smoke, in appearance, as it moved off; being dragged by the strong north wind, like that of a gutted belly heavy with tears of blackened sorrow.

And still searching for bodies amongst the charred shacks—Ricky Snakes felt an unevenness beneath his boot, as if he'd stepped on an overturned bowl OR a ball. But when he lifted his boot, looking up at him from the charred, damp debris was a grinning human skull. Its flesh, eyes, ears, nose, all gone (the facial tissue - being so soft, is the first to go). And after putting the skull inside a bag, along with its blackened torso—Ricky Snakes carried on with his search—pulling burnt bodies and jutting limbs out from under reeking stacks of corrugated sheeting, damp wood and asbestos.

And the worst thing Ricky Snakes ever experienced—besides the tortured screams of those burning alive—was the smell of a burnt corpse. He said it gives off a clinging, sickly taint - like nothing you can imagine. And as a rookie, you can't help but vomit the first time you breathe in that nauseating, sweet, putrid scent of burnt flesh. The smell SO TERRIBLE it stays with you, and even after a shower; the unpleasantness, it remains. And as a fireman you have to live with that—you go to bed and wake up with the smell of death in your nostrils. And sometimes the only thing to help alleviate the reek, is a cotton bud dipped in eucalyptus oil—dabbed up the nose.

And I'll never forget the time-served words of Ricky Snakes:

'Firefighters throughout the world are brothers, with one passion in mind, and that is to save lives, even if it means to throw down your own. There is an adrenalin rush like no other when you're on your way to an emergency call. Being a firefighter, is a calling, a special calling, it's not just a nine-to-five job, and whether you are on day leave, they can call you at any given time, be it by phone, radio or TV.'

17.

TOMBSTONE SKULL

FISHY flicked off my bed like a flea—meowing and scratching the bedroom door to be let out and investigate the noises in the house, as my dad went about his morning ritual.

And every morning Fishy would jump onto the basin counter and sit with purrs and turtle dove cooings to watch Ricky Snakes rake a hot blade of double-edge steel through cool cream: a face shaven clean for each new day—splashed fresh with Ice Blue, Aqua Velva.

* * *

The noises of an awakening day now stood around me *starkers* as I found it impossible to rest. The remnants of that drug driving dungeons through me... Catacombs of wanderlust - every possibility in shackles - detained in boarded-up vaults of desolation—leaving nothing but anxiety and a cold boredom within. The heavy debris that was once the fizzing glitters of bright hallucination and quivering ecstasy now nothing more than a pile of ash. My tombstone skull loud with whizzing chain-saws and grinding gears that whined relentless torment, a restless shudder. But within this fantastic moment - insightful downloads pinged wisdom, in which I realized, everything is word and action, horrible and full of wonder, as life lived in fear, is a watched pot left on the stove too long; all the goodness bombed out. Fear: the egos defiant default bearing. For a life lived in fear, is a life unlucky—no mometum what-so-ever. Fear: a gateway to decay. For what is life but a personalised game, and not anything to get all screwed-up about. So don't be killing yourself too much on perceived truths, I mean; freak out once in a while, you know. Release the tension in the brain, howl at the moon, whatever it takes. Take a trip *on the open road* OR within your mind, you know, that complete poetic *derangement of the senses* type-thang—losing yourself in the moment, in order to attract that wild, thrill-ride that ultimately like a magnet, exists to align, legendize and crown your soul.

And so, what is it all about, you might ask. For if it ain't about some eternal lesson, like an infinite loop of getting your ass kicked with each new Peekaboo! out the pussy portal, then perhaps it's just a gathering of data; missions and excursions to encode the DNA of future incarnations. The Origin (or Akashic) database recording each beings *evolution of consciousness* in transition (gaining experience), as abstract entities go between dimensions from 3rd to 5th via the 4th protocol - traversing this deathless cycle, being tried like silver purified seven times (in the furnace of life) on this physical plane Earth, to be ultimately transformed into a Diamond Soul of the ancient path.

* * *

Beneath the covers pulled up to my nose, I hid—wrapped in my four walls of anxiety. The stinging need to take a piss, overwhelming my brain, as eking its warmth into my bedroom window—the sun screeched its nails as it clawed all the way up a chalkboard sky—causing me to cringe and roll over in bed.

I waited for the house to clear. Zoë Snakes still getting ready for work (to run the Meals on Wheels center down the road)—having just risen, as per practice - swollen kneed, from deep, earnest prayers to the universe. Her thoughts, intentions, focus, words and elevated emotions—all for the opening of the storehouses of abundant and rich blessings from the astral realm. Zoë Snakes' firm belief that a submission to the present moment, through love and gratitude, attracted her charitable desires on a daily basis. Focus and intention the key to creating that beautiful life.

And then the house fell still.

I exited my bedroom with trepidation—checking all the rooms in my bowled-over state of paranoia—making sure no one was hiding under my parent's bed or behind the sofa or inside the wardrobes or kitchen cupboards—as in my frantic state of mind, I saw people darting about whenever I turned my back—changing hiding places - cos man-o-man was I in a state - totally freaked out. My mind playing tricks. For I feared that if I had been seen by a Homo Sapien - it would have caused a major *shift* in the Universe—an echo that would have rocked the collective psyche. For to have anyone look upon me in that STATE—especially if THEY'D looked into my eyes: dark and dilated, hollow and nowhere - gleaming vicious and reflecting a wildness that I'm sure if anyone saw this mid-phase mutation, it would have been a detriment - terrifying the living crap out of anyone, or so I imagined.

* * *

I opened the back door and Fishy bolted out like a wound-up spring released *BOING!*—inspecting the back garden where male cats had sprayed in the night - while barefoot on the damp lawn I paced up and down - the fresh morning sun stained-golden as it lined the edges of grass blades that shot harsh prickles between my toes. My sense of touch was not the same. Nerve endings numb as a sparkless fuse. I felt apart from myself - with all of Life's sweetness washed out - my "comedown" a trial of nerves. My nerve endings bitter and raw, as sucking sore-throated on my Joey Jim Blues—foolishly I tried piecing it all together—trying to come to terms with the significance of that night: the orange symbol, the self-harm, the incantations—nothing added up - the whole trip fucking mental.

I decided to set out for the day. But first I fried up a quick lentil patty and munched it between toast—washing it down with a mug of bitter black coffee. Then, locking the back door and security gate, I closed the windows—rubbed Fishy 'Goodbye x.'—and disappeared into Saratoka Plains for the whole deplorable day.

18.

SCARECHILD

AND usually, I'd have magical times in Saratoka Plains—stoned or sacredly gone—an entire world all to myself, as on many occasions at night, parked off and lit up by stars—young and filled with explosion of color THERE on the moon-washed banks of Bucks Dam—chilling with a "joint" smouldering sweetly between my fingers; with a head topped-up on "amarant"—I'd trip-out and adhere to the perfect scene of solitude—watching moonbeams plate ripples that glided mercury over rolling waters that moved dark like slow, heated wine. The heavy lake: enclosed by bare trees, that like guardians stood forked into the glowing violet sky: diluted by tower lights that hummed on mute watchful hills, as hitting another drag—soaking up that sweet, creamy intoxication: pungent as octopus ink—I'd hold it within my sea sponge lungs - until that burning sensation, and coughing violently, spit, and with eyes closed—feeling then proper goofed, I'd draw in a fresh breath of midnight and warble mesmeric – open to a whole new version of my surroundings—slowly picking out the encircling sounds: the sweet silvery purr of a cricket in the grass, the frenzied click from warty toads and prophylactic-throated frogs, the squabbling conversational honks from grouped ducks that boated by, and somewhere, on a hushed dirt road, within the magnetic darkness, a "Churring" sound—signifying the presence of the mythical and supernatural Nightjar - a bird as cute as slippers, but known also to steal milk from sleeping goats—who in surreptitious flight—is as erotically merciful as a virgin bride's blood engorged vulva - moist and succulent in the thrill of the big night - primed and hungry to be ball-slapped between some seedy, rundown motel's shit and bloodstained; serial killer walls. But now concerning this particular "come-down incident"—there was no compassion, or magic or pleasure present here, just the residue of that *visual drug* crackling within—denying me the chance to recuperate. For too afraid to be spotted by anyone, I felt the mutation had taken on it full form. The monster of my mind having come to life. This being no mental construct. For I have seen it before. SHOCK the catalyst for such grand mutations of the physical form. All due to a breakdown of the spiritual, emotional and mental well-being—remembering a childhood friend: Duffy Decastro. His sister, Jackie, got killed in a car crash. And at the shock of losing his beloved, Duffy's mind, and everything that made up the essence of Duffy, just went into full shut down mode. His brain sitting in his skull like smiling cheese. Yep, Duffy Decastro... A once jovial kid. Good with grades. Sharp like diamond dust—reduced to "a drooling simpleton". Poor Duffy Decastro, who got blindsided by life and got tossed down the mental straits of no return. A once upright, bristling being, altered into a gurn-faced monk. For it was a complete and radical transmutation. Even the scientists were baffled. Poor Master Decastro, a once silver stud boyo, who made girls squish hot with delicious juice. Yesss, believe - girls worshipped him. But after that nerve-crack, Duffy lost his hygiene, his teeth dropped out, and he developed a speech disorder.

And so they locked poor Duffy up in a bounce house for crazies. "A detriment to the outside world," they said—recalling one morning at the Seventh Seal Society Church: all us kids stood around broken glass edged in blood. And it was Duffy's blood. After a police investigation they confirmed the sad news: Duffy had broken into the church hall, teeth gnashing, as the sound of weeping echoed within his brain (as if every disembodied consciousness lost to Outer Darkness was locked inside his skull). It turned out that Duffy had gashed open his forearm—punching the window to climb inside and piece together his missing self. But Duffy's search proved fruitless—God was not to be found in church that day, if ever. And when the doctors released Duffy from the nut house; drugged on heavy meds, all he was good for was loitering supermarket car parks with head bowed; smiling at his own shoes, collecting trolleys while drooling on his work coat and giggling big wet goofy gums whenever he thought he heard his name being called.

And so now like a vile, desperate fella hung in chains of sacrifice, my thoughts rang bent-boned like echoing spells that glow in the dark—as dodging behind bushes, afraid to be looked upon and scrutinized like some new insect, the only comfort I found was within the environment. A bird resting in the sun on a branch - singing and flying off. A lizard cooling cat-eyed beneath succulent shade. A desolate breeze rustling in the dry blown grass. A black beetle on antenna legs stilting up a mound of loose sand - each tiny grain a treasure of matchless stone. Yesss. This little realm I could deal with. But that Homo sapien slave-trap of confusion - that iron clang of mean hearts and cold pride, pushed with rush squads that run wild, wide and headless—chasing a living to cut out a dream - yeah, I just couldn't take that bullshit.

*　*　*

And so now, deep inside my being—I knew something had unequivocally been tampered with. A rewiring or reformation of some kind—something life changing having been proposed, as now with hyenas laughing in the highest tower of my mind, and crying jackals in the pleasant places of my soul: a collective of beasts howling in the deepest crypt of my being—there I stood—a sacred freak, a spiritual treasure chosen to rove the earth like a god - wounded by the mark of my very own pact.

And as I lay there with this fizzing realization, waiting to be struck with an alternative idea, nothing arose. Therefore; right then and there, I made up my mind. I consciously chose to be the Rebel Scarechild I was born to be. Burning bright like the morning sun—kicking up gravy delight for everyone.

* * *

It was evident that the Universe's original plan for me had been scrapped. Replaced by a whole new modus operandi. My old self, a distant prototype, a shadow well used, had been tossed away like some rusty tampon, having served its purpose well: inserted into this platform of time to soak up the bloodiness of hard livings—until the appointed time.

* * *

It was time to commence as though it were the first day of my life - a newborn materializing into this platform of life, flopping out the portal—after having been pickled in amniotic juices for nine sweet months.

19.

ROCCA DEL CULTO

I returned home about 8 pm. Since early afternoon I'd been in Saratoka Plains, pacing about (muttering under-breath some hot 'n' cold meander) the day's light fading each second, as stretched to confusion - spread on guilt—I hovered lost after having being spiritually raped by that ginormous, flaming monster cock. My soul sucked hollow and creampied with a steaming hot load of cum.

The seal had been set in place. The Book of Life open on its rightful page. I had been called upon now to fulfill my life's contract—recalling the struggles of my hero: Rocca del Culto—the Kiawana bluester legend with slicked-back hair—wearing his signature felt hat and biting a cigar—who, while leaned-up against a rock—dying from snakebite, laid it down with slide guitar, as he cried out that number one hit: 'Beggars Door'—wailing: "I met The Man at the cross in the road ... I signed the line with my blood, skull and bones ... I found myself in a goldmine ... I lost my head it was dynamite ... Those golden rays of the sun gonna make you feel real good. I was born and raised ready to burn ... I took the beggars door to heaven ... Now I am a criminal taking names ... People I turn on just turn to flames ... Cos not only a loser knows just what it feels ... To feel like dirt."

And then, having moaned his last words of sincerity—Rocca del Culto, in true legend style, rested back his head and died—giving his soul over to the other side.

And so with thoughts of Rocca del Culto hot on my mind, like him, I knew I was born to ride the outrage, as mad to run with it, and go out brightly lit, I hid my face in my hands.

28.

REST IN PEACE OLD FRIEND

OPENING the front door I stepped inside house №13.

My mother was doing the ironing while the TV played sport highlights.

She greeted me. I tried acting my normal self. But couldn't. It was far too late. For the moment my mother said my name (in her usual loving manner) I realized the person my parents knew as their son, was no longer alive. For in this awakening (I understood) that a part of me had been removed and had been replaced, although, not completely, just yet. A slight pinprick of sentiment still glowing. A remnant of my former self: the old data, fighting back - as like a low, grieving flame at the back of my mind—memories of a childhood lingered: red tinted days that exploded sad, happy glowings of my shadow self. Them great sad, lost days of delusion and family silence at the meal table. The image of my gentle-Jezem mother; the one I held before my soul death, shining like a Mother Madonna. Oh, momma dear momma, the one who gave me life, and taught me Jezem Jainko, and the alphabet - MY MOTHER: the soul of her heavenly face preserved in Instamatic color. The snapshot of her pegging washing on the line in the hot midday sun, forever burnt into my brain. She being my first girl. My first heartache head rush, dressed in hot pants, a red v-neck tee and brown leather sandals. Body firm and as healthy as a chestnut mare with long, shiny black hair. Oh, youthful mother, my endless love. My beautiful Lakashte "first girl"—what happened to us? Our loving days—when you were like a sister - in times when it was enough to get by on simple struggles. But yet - weren't we all so asleep back then. Those times of innocence and ignorance, when God answered my good prayer in the night - the one you taught me that went: "Gentle Jezem, meek and mild, look upon every child, God bless Mommy and Daddy ... amen."

And so *now* realizing that my world before: of church and Jezem Jainko and guilt was built on an innocent lie - the moment my mother said my name - my new reality shook me to the core. I had to accept that my world had been changed forever - I had to accept it. No longer would be I the same blind person the system had indoctrinated and enslaved. For in my search of self, I had slain an old friend: my shadow self, who was in fact my enemy—a curse like an old love letter nailed to the heart - a sentimental relic, heavy as a millstone. For in my search for SELF, I had invited a bitter truth (a higher consciousness) to reside. It seemed like a bittersweet finality, even though it was a complete victory - my ego *obviously* still trying to pin me down with definitives. But if you wanna take on a dream—sometimes you gotta stake your life on the risks.

Rest in peace, old friend.
RIP It Up!

21.

MORE LUCID AND MAGICAL THAN EVER

EXISTING now with this new "Life" inside, the tide of inspiration broke me upon new sun-kissed apparitions. Things in a short spell growing more lucid and magical than ever. But then three years down the line—and the glowing embers of my so-called love affair with my "muse" began to wane. The burstings for a new gig to spark me whole again, rising up—paralleled with things aplenty that worked me down:

First, Fishy got run over. It was too sad - in minutes of me spending time with her; full of life, she was dead. And so hunched over Fishy's lifeless body, there was not a mark on her, just a trickle of blood from a nostril. And when I placed her in the cold belly of the earth, she was still warm. It was a shock. I never cried - was just angry. A day or two later, though, I broke down into a depression. My furry friend was gone. I felt numb, all welled up with heartsore sorrow I could not express.

And so as it goes, such counterbalances they swung to settle the scores of karmic ripples and whirlpools. My life falling upon the crossing line of spiritual equators. Trials such as heartache and cold flames. The ruthless and cunning sex machine, Sapphire; addictive as a drug, doing me wrong—or perhaps I just misread the sparks in her eyes - although you never can tell with enchanting women, they are as brutal as fuck—for they'll get you all caught up believing the pain in your heart is love, when meantime it's the motherfucking spear in your back that's sticking out your chest. That's why you gotta be proper on your game - cos if you asleep, you'll get damaged. But hey, regardless, such women are a vital force of nature, they're like a firestorm that once you've passed through - you return (to yourself) a stronger, wiser man.

And other than that—"Happy-days"—my mother of all people, she cut down my prized weed tree. That thing producing the best smoke ever - until one day I come home, only to find my baby all neatly chopped to pieces and tied up into black bags - ready for the garbage truck. Maaan, was I pissed. My own mother saying I was getting out of hand. Bringing home ragged, drunken, hobo women to smash. Their screams of abandon waking up my snoring folks in the "middles of the night"— lying awake till morning - listening to my pump; worrying— wondering what had become of their once well-behaved son.

Now at this juncture I was unemployed. Not that I cared for work, or had the desire to float up the "ranks" of working class stardom like ambitious scum. But in this dog-lick-dog-ass world, if you wanna roll hot - *ca-ching* is paramount—especially if you wish to score good drugs and fuck righteous pussy. And so, as life would have it - stuck again, living off pocket money from my folks (not much)—just enough to buy smokes, rolling papers and the odd bottle of dreg wine, I found myself having to hock unloved "reads" to second-hand bookstores *for cash-in-hand*, just so I could score some more of dat *Sweet Baby Sunshine:* Mercia Gold—or if she wasn't on the market, I'd settle for her sista, dat shaweet purple-cloud-electric Eskia Green - in support of my ever growing dependency on the psychological fogs and perceptual depths, brought on by the intense sensory shift of being immaculately stoned. Yep, my life became a scrounger's get by—and on occasion; when I could pull a job—it was cleaning typewriters in classrooms across the region, again, cash-in-hand, 70 buckskins a day.

Then in late 1998, I managed to get a steadier income— working as a rides operator at Al'Limo Junction—"The Wildest Place In Māratopia", or that's how they sold it. A rollercoaster theme park for cheap thrill enthusiasts. And at the time it was a big thing in Māratopia, and provided jobs for many layabout youngsters, unable to get work that matched their qualifications in Māratopia's job-scarce climate.

This was also now around about the time I started dating my cousin, who had a 7-year-old kid, who, one-day accused me of looking at him funny. So things couldn't get any better. After all, I wasn't ready to be no role model yet. But here this kid was, literally family, doting all over me, trying to match warmth and shit. But I knew I wouldn't be around much longer—his mom and I just fucking our way toward a split, you know; testing the fates and all. And so it kinda felt weird - he looking up to me like I was gonna roll out some red carpet filled with fond 'ol daddy times. I mean; talk about claustrophobic, huh! Hence I didn't want him holding my hand like I was some paternal foundation he could build love on. The situation was warped beyond repair, cos (in truth) I was hooked blind, you could say, by that fat juicy toad between my cousin's thighs. For by golly, when I plugged my manhood inside my cuzz—merging as one flesh—*KA-BAM!*—I experienced a falling that took me deeper into any woman's soul than anyone I've ever been apart of. And not only that... The part of her body, which I ate like fruit, it tasted good. Her juice, the juice of my ancestors. For in tasting my cousin, I received a renewed spirit. A gush of neurochemical-revival that roused my brain into a wild space - blasting out all my energy blockages - making me see suns and moons and shooting stars - as, ahhhh, yes, indeed - my love for my cousin became a drug. I had always been in love with her though. I dreamt of our nakedness together: caressing, holding, melting and soft, wet kissing. Thought she was the most beautiful woman in the whole wide world; next to my own mother. And I guess through connecting with my cousin I was working out something heavy - dealing with some deep shit buried hardcore within my subconscious - relating to my formative years *when* as a boy's I be star-struck smitten by my own mother, who became my everything.

Down in the pit of my stomach though, despite the

possibility that we could have made the relationship work, I knew it was dead. Hitting pure core, with both of us having found no diamonds - the nicety of the situation between me and my cousin had begun to cramp our style as individuals.

And so after refusing a promotion at my first job at Orion Star Shipping in 1995—telling Mr. White, my manager, to stuff it—when his terms were: I cut my hair and give up smoking weed, I kinda fell out of society. For at age-20—nothing was more important than writing poetry, getting high, and growing my hair. Besides, I didn't think a waste-of-time job was a profitable distraction - considering my investment into my future as King Poet extraordinaire. But after three years unemployed, and sweetly screwing my cousin (each night like easy pickings)—reality hit like pigeon shit on a door knob. As no longer was I facing "a little bit of fun"—for it was now A WOMAN who had serious plans (for the both of us). A woman plotting our life together - all this being conditional—this eventual future that she foresaw for the both of us, only manifesting *if and when* I woke up and got with the trend: a job, a haircut, my own accommodation; plus a complete overhaul of character: adopting that sour ignorance, mixed in with arrogance that married people acquire after the sex turns into a stale habit—you know; those nicely polished people with sedated "I'm so pleased with my life" self-absorbed grins, as if they'd never taken a shit in their entire life. Therefore; it came as a little confidence-knocker - the fact that all her friends had good jobs, cool cars, big homes, and were all feeling great about their abundant lives. Meanwhile, like some dedicated shitheel, I was still jobless - living with "mommy and daddy"—which meant it was all up to my poor cousin to supply condoms, and pay for drinks, and restaurant meals on romantic evenings out - added to the humiliation of getting moaned at by her across the *tables* of these so-called; what were meant to be, romantic dinners. The main topic of outburst being my lazy approach to our relationship, and just life in general, which made me feel both a little angry and helpless. She treating me like her pet project.

Although in saying that - I did owe much to my cousin, she, partially right. It's just the way she came across at the time, that's all, you know - unrefined and pushing my buttons. And so as a result, instead of me taking her crass advice, I behaved stupidly - I sulked like a fool - my pride somewhat bruised by her raw wisdom. The big pressure from her: that I make something of myself, when in fact I was no way near any stage of high maintenance development or realisation of who I was in the pecking order of the rat race. All that competiton-based anxiety was not for me. I had enough on the table just trying to be a young poet and all, and questioning myself, gaslighting myself, that just seemed non-productive. But being so deeply attached to a worldly woman, giving her what she wanted, plus not wanting to sell out, caused me to feel a bit lost, for being Piscian, I like to evolve buzzing within my own intuition. And furthermore, I don't take kindly when my insight gets discredited over decisions acted on in fear; instead of heart felt choice. But yeah, I do get it, she was only being that way to raise our status as a couple, I guess. But regardless, her attitude was short-sighted and uncalled for. After all, already I felt bad enough, and was trying my utmost to be a man. But somehow though, I just couldn't lift myself out from the dumps - made lame with insecure feelings that I was nothing more to her than a fuck up. My fault though, as I kind of placed her on a pedestal.

And so this time of crisis, was around three months prior to the season our relationship soured. The time I got poisoned by her pussy—shitting black fluid and shaking sweats on the toilet.

I remember it all too well. It came like a backstabbing dagger in the dark - cold, fast and followed by a sputtering death. She, having two-timed me on a rainy night—having allowed this dude, Chad: a blonde Adonis with a Viking-beard and hungry eyes to fuck her pussy. The guy living in the same ten-bedroom house as her (in the bedsit next door). I never like him. He was sophisticated, cool and handsome - a shit-talking alpha with a job, car and a laptop - a proper chick magnet. And after they did it - Chad went back to his room and she fell asleep; hair soaked in sweat, the way he smashed up her pussy (all too well).

And for some reason, that night, I suffered insomnia. My heart pounding palpitations. For I had visions of the truth. And in my restlessness I jumped on my bike and raced frantically through the rain like an idiot whose time had run out—pedaling like a chimp in a cheap circus show. And when I got there, I climbed up onto her balcony, pulled back the sliding door, slipped under the covers and began to eat her out (as she slept)—and with that dude's sea-juice still leaking from her pussy; before I knew it, I had swallowed a mouthful of nicotine-flavored semen (the smell of man all over her skin like homeless juice). And all this mix-up of insecurities, limp dick feelings and nasty livings was due to not having a job or mega bucks rolling in. As most times, I guess, it's all about providing a secure zone for your woman to sink into. So guys, learn a thread or two about how your women needs knowing her man is taking care of "things"— putting in the time and sweat to earn dem buckskins righteous; in order to make life flow. I mean; if you wanna make life easy; living with a woman - just drip feed her the right amount of money, enough that she can spend without a care in the world, and guaranteed, you'll be getting the sweetest sex whenever you want - even if she's on her bloodiest month or shrivelled up with cob webs; she'll be putting out till the day you die - just like a whore on a steady payroll; only thing is, is that she'll be your whore, your queen, your bitch. And so that's how, operating off that cool-headed heat, you will make that sweet prize open up like a pretty piece of delicate meat. Hence the reason why I recall my first job with fondness:

22.

THE PLAYGROUND

1994, I began work as a filing clerk for Orion Star Shipping—Māratopia's oldest shipping company. And after about a week, I received my first ever wage. My jeans bulging with a little manilla pay packet—stuffed with notes and coins, as in that late afternoon haze, strutting homeward, I had my first taste of independence. Officially I was a workingman now, and boy did it feel good.

At the proud age of 20, I still lived with my folks. But at least now, on a wage, I didn't need to sponge money from them—and more importantly, I could focus on saving the amount needed to get my poetry into print.

But before anything - it was imperative that I got back the time a week of inane bullshit, numbskullery work had robbed me of. And so the perfect place to get a full night-of-flight into my bloodstream, was at a nightclub on L'Shasta Street named, The Playground.

The Playground was the perfect paradise for the obsequious drug fiend - its interior resembling a commune for psychonauts: the blackened, labyrinthine rooms, the psychedelic artwork, the low ceilings, the shrine-like murals on the walls - making it the perfect place to 'trip' and freak out.

But before I entered The Playground (first thing) from the cellophane outer skin on my Joey Jim Blues, I took the drugs-cash set aside for such an instance—slippin' the leathery red note into the clammy hand of a drug merchant, who went by the name: Selvin.

Sold at 50 buckskins a 'trip'—all Selvin had in his possession were double-dipped Neon Chimeras (blotter "amarant") wrapped in foil paper: the size of a pinkie fingernail.

And so, heading down a quiet, lonely street—below a biscuit-faced moon that covered the entire night's sky - I wedged the "amarant" under my tongue and grumbled my mantra: "See you on the other side". And then, back-tracking it to L'Shasta Street—paying the 10 buckskins admission—I got a rubber stamp across my wrist—and entered The Playground.

* * *

Lost in intrigue like a boy beneath the bed covers reading his favorite dark comic book by torch light—I took it all in. The Playground, everything, the church warned me against. It had drugs, suggestive music, sluts, bad company, temptations, dark presence - you name it—it was the perfect place for a young impressionable poet like me.

Up a spiral stair and onto a diamond plate platform - crossing a wooden suspension bridge that broke off into a tiger's cage, there I found a leopard print sofa and stretched out across it. My blood oozing through my veins like bubbling jam as firing up a fat doob I dragged FULSOME hits—my ears ringing high-pitched blood and my heart pounding stampedes that knocked my chest out - when *FUTHOOM!* a blood-bursting, hot-razzling charge spiked right through me as I stood, dead in a daze. And then without warning, another intense wave of the drug hit me with a thunderclap that nearly knocked me off my feet *KA-POW!* as stumbling over the suspension bridge, all the way down the spiral staircase, I staggered like a drunkard—as again, without mercy *FA-LASH!* an earth shuddering pulse electrifying my senses shot up from my feet, through my legs, all along my body and into my brain with a blast that made me buzz insane with an intense rush of desire to explode.

THE PLAYGROUND

Whatever was happening, it sure felt like heart-sized hydrogen bombs were going off inside - images rapid, bursting into inexpressible beauty—everything appearing to be spun out of intense neon, as in no time - teleported - I found myself atop of that spiral staircase—gradually making my way back down again. My brains were cooked. Electri-fried fish paste *if you will* when abruptly *K-RAK!* I got hit by a wave of psychosis - the patriarchal eye of my brain burning a watchful judgment on my actions; a nervous breakdown in the making, as in strobing snatches, I caught myself holding my head like a nut, scurrying through the nightclub in zigzags—trying to locate the exit, lost, going totally insane, while from nowhere, a menacing chorus began looping through my head - sounding like some crazed *on-the-rise* mean steam-driven calliope - enveloped in apocalyptic flames of ridicule.

And in that protracted moment, all I wished for was solace - dreaming of sucking on some big racy titties while ejaculating in my nappies like a newborn; embraced and sheltered from the non-stop chaos in my head. But no chance. For it seemed I had already locked antlers with the moment—and was set to ride it through - until its dire end.

* * *

I couldn't remember a thing. Who I was. My name. Even what I was doing there—the perfect platform for rebirth. But at this junction, not fully cognisant of the mechanics of the Universe, I desperately wanted to be me again—my ego in need of validation—everything just slipping away, the madness impossible to track, as now in wanting everything to go back to normal, I shouted out: "Please, make it stop!' waiting for the Universe to respond. But nothing. Absolutely fuck all. My nowhere state of mind reflected back upon myself, the Universe only capable of giving as long as I could see. But I could not see a thing. And should have know better. But in that time frame -

I knew nothing - had no connection to anything—for nobody heard my cry that night. The Universe didn't even bother to hiccup.

Then, through some ant-like sense of direction, I found myself outside The Playground. I froze—gazing down the street—everything now appearing shop-floor shiny and squeaky clean: a scintillation that glistened with ice-packed freshness, as even the dirty gutters shone—while in the tarmac patterns formed - each tiny gravel stone flashing with sharp, brilliant diamond-cut color that twisted and shot sparkles everywhere.

I then began going up to people. And on that night, I shook hands with many a stranger. And in all of them, each beautiful human car crash, I saw their own version of me; the shock and wonder of being trapped in mortal flesh, a delicate expression of trouble on the run. As each beautiful soul now, like a flower, navigating this minefield that is life - owned their own evolution floating through the river of existence - flowing like glowing students—all of us grabbing that opportunity to shift while feeling everything and everyone like we were already gone; yet somehow *safe*, headed to the great Candy Store of the Universe to pin our wishes and declare that we "Want some!" - taking our share of LIFE—with all the trimmings and colors possible.

Then suddenly - a sharp insight snagged my mind. A slippage of gold truth dipped in black goo had me locked big-eyed in a stare that said my candles had been blown out. As stood dumb below the molten moon I saw humankind for what it was: the avatar: a complex bio-tech bound in the entropic loop of a dark ruleset that has turned our vessels into nothing more than a rack of squeaky bones and organs burping mucus; draped in dying flesh.

And so I carried on as such - understanding that "the destroyer and creator of worlds" was observing life through me - wearing my skull like a fucking mask, while having a laugh at the same time, in pretending to be me. The consciousness or awareness or whatever is in each and every one of us, nothing but a fucking shit worm who just can't help feeding off us. And even though I cracked it - the fact we really don't exist at all—or at least don't exist from a physical standpoint, I saw there was only one purpose for living: to be observed. Yep, the only reason why we are here, is to be studied like a fucking turd in a jar.

And for a moment I had to pull myself back from the lunatic *two-thousand-yard stare* of a Universe that was blowing my mind with such *ideas for ideas* - as now drawing toward myself; getting a slim sense of direction, I saw every single face that came toward me now as a mirror that rotted slowly before my eyes. Each pore a septic sulfurous geyser that spewed death. Bodies oiled in sweat that slid sick with a humming taint as aloof-in-oblivion like big tits they bounced - heads held high in keeping up their end of the lie with everyday smiles worn like warped masks that hid the permanent grimace that screamed beneath.

* * *

I stared into the blackness above, a web of shimmering rivets like a holy carousel of light illuminating my face, as shooting by, a comet cut through the sad junk of mortal livings—disappearing to that place where wild dreams run fast, free and rampant.
From standing lost in the middle of the street, I retreated into a crypt-hollow doorway, and closing my eyes, tuned-in to the voices that rustled in the dying distance - voices that twisted upwards like voodoo smoke—familiar voices sent out like praises to the guardian spirits of the open road.

'At the crossroads again, huh? murmured a voice. Well, you never learn, do you,' it croaked. 'What's it gonna be this time. What you gonna give, and what promises you gonna make to get yourself outta this one?'

And on the outside, to any passer-by not prepared for the sight of seeing a fellow being "fantastically smashed"—I must have appeared catatonic: burnt up and dragged down. But this was all a ruse, a cloaking devise. For on the inside - that was where the treasure lay. Fireworks of Fortune—my life's grand oration struck like a nemesis rock. My communication with the guardians, and what they did impart: a colossal delivery of supernatural proportions - a masterful stroke, a cool hoodwink and a salute to the Universe—a super spectacle no one would ever see or hear—a fleeting disclosure of a fugitive dream—machinations of double-dealing, both tragedy and ecstasy, as pleading promises to myself Higher self, at the same time, I made backstage pacts with my ego.

Next day—morning till sundown, I lay in bed like a lame man tormented by nightmarish flashbacks and sparkling episodes of teleportation. And come nightfall, Léguvan paid me a visit. I told him all about my "amarant" trip. And it worried him. He said I was preparing for a big fall. And he was right; maybe. But come Monday—walking to work, I fired-up a biggie and chugged it all the way—playing out my last days on the job at Orion Star Shipping.

23.

MAD MICKY NOLAN

EVENTUALLY, I broke it off with my cuz. That "night-of-nights" sucking on her vag; soaked in another man's seed—made me think big about what I wanted from life. And so mulling it over, taking a spill; drowned in Deadman's whiskey - within a hard-hearted second, I was square over her. That scar across my heart pushing me to look for a job down in Lomita Town, South East, Māratopia County. These trials all taking place in 1998, when I was still going around with the glass-eyed poet/surfer Mad Micky Nolan, who had a lizard tattooed on his left foot and ears pierced like a pirate. Yep, good ole Mad Micky Nolan, who with dog manners, would piss all over toilet seats in the homes of those he thought (in his schizoid mind) were out to get him—never to be invited back of course. But that was Mad Micky Nolan through and through. He drew lines when others would have just eaten shit and burned in anger.

Short and articulate with long blonde dreads—Mad Micky Nolan had his sister's striking blues. And two years before we met, he'd almost died in a car crash—losing one eye and a grip on reality. The horror, touching him up with a glitch on the brain. Mad Micky Nolan at times—blanking out cold, often sat cross-legged by wood fire on the beach, as most times (together) we'd spend (like this)—smoked-up on some of the best strains of weed—charged on Wild Maker Tequila or whatever brand of booze Mad Micky Nolan could pinch from the bar at Arrowhead backpacking Lodge, where he worked as a barman—sleeping on the front lawn - his home, a humble 2-man tent.

And so—after witnessing Mad Micky Nolan blackout (many a time) - it dawned, "Damn!" the poor guy had already died in that car crash. And was now just a living ghost—haunting my life and the lives of all those closest to him.

But what can I say, I was hooked on Mad Micky Nolan - his one-eye and quirky ways. Somehow we filled each other's need for companionship in the short span we spent together as burning buds - for most of his and my friends, we'd lost—being unconcerned about saving face or minding what we said in order to present a false reality. And most people don't like hanging about people like this—they call you names like: "madman", or "badman" or "fool", or even "crazy". That's why during that time, to everyone, we both were dead men.

And so after having not heard from Mad Micky Nolan for well over a year; Mad Micky Nolan having made his own plans to venture into the North Eastern Region of Māratopia and rough-it - out of the blue, I received a postcard from Grizzly Tooth Territory, beyond the treacherous Wolfdern Forest. And it revealed that Micky had sunken down roots in this remote area of Māratopia County, and was now living as a cactus/fruit seller—trading in peyote, mango, guava, chayote and prickly pear. And from his good money he bought a plot of land, built a house (made of clay), and got engaged to a Changa hottie.

 And so every three weeks, with word from the outskirts, I'd sprawl over Mad Micky Nolan's midnight oil postcards—dreaming of finding my own high tan hottie - inspired like a man with a new vision, as I made my final preparations for Lomita Town.

The End

www.ingramcontent.com/pod-product-compliance
Lightning Source LLC
Chambersburg PA
CBHW071203070526
44584CB00019B/2897